Understanding Financial Statements

A Primer of Useful Information

Revised Edition

James O. Gill
Moira Chatton

A Fifty-Minute™ Series Book

CRISP PUBLICATIONS, INC.
Menlo Park, California

Understanding Financial Statements

A Primer of Useful Information

Revised Edition

James O. Gill
Revised by Moira Chatton

CREDITS:
Editor: **L.K. Woodbury**
Senior Editor: **Debbie Woodbury**
Production Manager: **Judy Petry**
Text Design: **Amy Shayne**
Cover: **Amy Shayne and Fifth Street Design**
Cartoons: **Ralph Mapson**
Production Artist: **Robin Strobel**

© 1990, 1999 Crisp Publications, Inc.
Printed in the United States of America by Von Hoffmann Graphics, Inc.

CrispLearning.com

00 01 02 03   10 9 8 7 6 5 4 3 2

Library of Congress Catalog Card Number 99-74177
Gill, James and Moira Chatton
Understanding Financial Statements, Revised Edition
A Primer of Useful Information
ISBN 1-56052-425-1

This book is printed on recyclable paper with soy ink.

Learning Objectives For:

Understanding Financial Statements

The objectives for *Understanding Financial Statements* are listed below. They have been developed to guide you, the reader, to the core issues covered in this book.

OBJECTIVES

☐ 1) To describe how the three primary financial statements are prepared and what each means to a business.

☐ 2) To explain the differences between cash and profit from an accrual prospective.

☐ 3) To introduce ratios and proportions and show how easily they are developed and used.

☐ 4) To explain how to examine and get better productivity from your expenses.

☐ 5) To provide tested techniques for gaining better control over your business finances.

ASSESSING YOUR PROGRESS

In addition to the learning objectives, Crisp, Inc. has developed an **assessment** that covers the fundamental information presented in this book. A twenty-five item, multiple choice/true-false questionnaire allows the reader to evaluate his or her comprehension of the subject matter. An answer sheet with a chart matching the questions to the listed objectives is also available. To learn how to obtain a copy of this assessment please call: **1-800-442-7477** and ask to speak with a Customer Service Representative.

Assessments should not be used in any selection process.

About the Authors

The late James O. Gill worked as Division Manager and Projects Manager with the Naval Weapons Support Center in Crane, Indiana. He was the author of *Financial Basics of Small Business Success, Financial Analysis,* and the first edition of *Understanding Financial Statements,* all published by Crisp Publications, Inc. Jim enjoyed great success teaching financial basics to people with limited financial backgrounds.

The new author selected to revise *Understanding Financial Statements* is Moira E. Chatton. She earned a degree in biochemistry from the University of California, Berkeley, and an M.B.A. from the University of Georgia. Employed initially as a financial analyst by Chevron Chemical Company in San Francisco, she held a series of increasingly responsible and challenging positions in other Chevron companies.

Since retiring from Chevron, Ms. Chatton provides in-house financial training to local businesses and teaches small business and finance courses at Santa Rosa Junior College and the University of Phoenix.

Preface

This is a reference manual designed to help increase your understanding of your business. The material is not complex, but will take some time to master. It is suggested that you first skim through the book to gain an overview of the material and then start from the beginning. Progressing through the book and using the blank forms to work up your own ratios and percentages will give you a level of comfort. By the time you have completed this book, you should understand control techniques that you can use in your business.

There is no need to memorize the contents of this book. More emphasis should be placed on thinking about your business as you develop and compare ratios. The page-by-page layout of ratios (and other tools) will enable you to refer to those that are significant to your business at the time you want to use them. Not all of the ratios and techniques were meant to be used every time you check on the health of your business or determine a future strategy, but you should be aware of those most applicable to your situation.

You will be introduced to twelve standard ratios. As a general rule, several will be meaningful once a month, others will be important once a year. Still others will be useful as your business grows. These ratios are for you to apply when they are right for you. There is no hard and fast rule when to use ratios. They are simply tools that can help you succeed.

It is important for every business owner and employee to understand where a business is making money and where it is not. This is the function of finance. By applying the fundamentals of financial planning and decision making, you can make more money during good times and lose less during bad periods.

Understanding Financial Statements will teach you the basics, but will not make you an expert. It will help to clear up some misunderstandings about finance but will not make you a CPA. It simply gives you some tools that will help you understand your financial statements and help you predict and control the future of your business.

Contents

PART 4: HOW TO PERFORM A RATIO ANALYSIS

PART 5: HOW TO PERFORM AN EXPENSE ANALYSIS

PART 6: HOW TO CONTROL YOUR BUSINESS

INTRODUCTION

This revised edition of *Understanding Financial Statements* is written for all business owners, managers and employees who want better control and understanding of the business they manage or work for. In this era of downsizing, outsourcing and contracting, owners, managers and employees must understand the financial aspects of the business in which they work to perform effectively on the job today and lead their businesses into the 21st century.

Over half of all new businesses (excluding franchises) fail within four years. Another 30 percent don't last 10 years. Many of the survivors stay alive, but stagnate without reaching their full potential. Often, a lack of capital is cited as the reason a business failed. This reason is often true of potentially successful businesses that have no trouble obtaining customers. Ironically, quick but uncontrolled success has caused the downfall of thousands of businesses because owners and managers were unaware of the financial reasons behind their success and blindly over-expanded.

Understanding Financial Statements is a first step for all business owners and employees on how to use financial information to better understand, monitor and interpret the operations of their businesses. This edition places even greater emphasis on cash and cash flow projections to make sure that owners and managers know where their business is going. It is not highly technical and it is *not* a complete text on financial analysis. You'll be introduced to a balance sheet, an income statement and a cash flow statement. You'll learn how to interpret these statements and use financial ratios to evaluate business performance.

IT IS GOOD BUSINESS TO UNDERSTAND BASIC FINANCE.

P A R T 1

The Basics of

Financial Statements

What Are Financial Statements and Who Uses Them?

It is a fact that the lack of growth or failure of a business often comes from over-buying, over-trading or over-expanding. For example, a lumber yard significantly increased sales for three straight years then failed. Why? Because the owner couldn't resist a bargain. He over-bought too much of too many items that were offered with volume discounts. He used up so much cash that his on-going expenses, such as rent, utilities and salaries couldn't be paid on time. Similarly, a plastics manufacturer had a modern, labor-saving plant, well-stocked inventory and increasing sales. But this same manufacturer had to let go of some ownership because a current loan could not be paid. Why? Because sales were obtained by offering loose credit terms and discounts. Business can avoid these *cash flow traps* by doing a good job of financial analysis.

The difference between failure and success is not always the lack of product knowledge or of failing to put in long hours. More often it is not understanding the financial situation. Because new businesses usually have financial reports prepared by someone in the family or by a CPA, owners or managers often do not understand the financial implications and make poor choices. Even in large, publicly-traded corporations, accounting or finance departments frequently prepare financial reports and often managers do not know how to use them.

Financial statements are the principal means of reporting financial information to people within an organization—management and other employees—and to people outside an organization—banks, investors, suppliers and others.

Publicly-traded corporations must comply with strict requirements for financial statement reporting. Generally Accepted Accounting Principles (GAAP) are the "ground rules" for financial reporting. They provide the framework for what information is included in financial statements and how the information should be presented. They are designed so that financial statement information about businesses is reliable and comparable.

To have a functional understanding of finance, it is essential to thoroughly understand balance sheets, income statements and cash flow statements. In this section, we will review these three important financial statements.

The Balance Sheet

A company's financial position or *health* is shown on the balance sheet, also called the statement of condition or statement of financial position. It shows the business's financial position *on a particular date*.

The typical balance sheet displays the business's assets on the left side of the page and liabilities and net worth on the right side like this:

Debt = Credit

BALANCE SHEET		
Assets	=	Liabilities + Net Worth

Assets are normally *debit balances* and are what a business *owns*. Assets are broken into two main categories: current assets and fixed assets. **Current assets** usually mean anything that can be converted into cash within one year. **Fixed assets**, often called long term assets, are more permanent items like buildings and major equipment.

Liabilities are normally *credit balances* and are what a business *owes*. Liabilities are divided into two main categories just like assets. They are shown as current liabilities (that which is owed within one year) and long term debt. **Current liabilities** include bills for such items as included in accounts payable, inventory, rent, salaries, etc. **Long term debt** includes items that by agreement do not need to be paid back quickly, such as a mortgage or long term note.

The difference between assets and liabilities equals **net worth**, which is often called stockholders' equity for publicly-traded corporations. That is, after all the bills and notes are paid, anything left over is called net worth. Another definition is that net worth is what is due the owner(s)/stockholders of the business once all liabilities have been paid.

Assets – Liabilities = Net Worth
or
Assets = Liabilities + Net Worth

The Balance Sheet (CONTINUED)

Why is it called a "Balance Sheet"?

The key word is *balance*. Because the total assets equal the total liabilities plus the net worth. This is true even if the liabilities exceed the assets. In this case, net worth becomes negative and it must be subtracted from the liabilities, instead of being added.

A balance sheet uses the principle of double entry accounting. It is called double entry because each business action affects two or more accounts. For example, a sale will increase cash or accounts receivable but decrease inventory. An account can be cash, inventory, money you owe (*accounts payable*), or owed to you (*accounts receivable*), etc. Accounts payable and accounts receivable are called *accrual* accounts. The balances in these accounts represent cash that must be *paid to* suppliers or will be *received from* customers at some future time.

Accounts are organized on the balance sheet in categories with current and fixed assets on the left side of the sheet and current and long term liabilities as well as net worth on the right side of the sheet. Remember, assets and liabilities plus net worth must always balance. A glossary of basic balance sheet terms is provided on pages 7 and 8 for easy reference.

Let's suppose that a new business was started with the owner's savings of $100,000. The beginning balance sheet would look something like this:

ASSETS		LIABILITIES + NET WORTH	
CURRENT ASSETS			
Cash	$100,000	Net Worth	$100,000

The owner then decides to stock her store, and purchases $50,000 of merchandise (**Inventory**), but pays only $25,000 in cash (this will reduce **Cash** by $25,000) and promises to pay the other $25,000 in thirty days (this creates a new account called Accounts Payable) which is placed under the category of Current Liabilities because the bill must be paid within one year. The balance sheet would now look like the example on the next page.

ASSETS		LIABILITIES + NET WORTH	
CURRENT ASSETS		**CURRENT LIABILITIES**	
Cash	$ 75,000	Accounts Payable	$ 25,000
Inventory	$ 50,000	Net Worth	$ 100,000
Total	**$ 125,000**	**Total**	**$ 125,000**

The balance sheet is in balance with the addition of $25,000 that is owed to the vendor. It is placed under current liabilities because it is due to be paid back in a specified period of time which is less than one year. Currents assets are those items that can be converted into cash within a year.

Now let's suppose that the owner buys a building for $100,000. She puts $25,000 down and obtains a $75,000 mortgage for the remainder.

The balance sheet would now look like this:

BALANCE SHEET			
CURRENT ASSETS		**CURRENT LIABILITIES**	
Cash	$ 50,000	Accounts Payable	$ 25,000
Inventory	$ 50,000		
Total Current Assets	**$ 100,000**	**Total Current Liabilities**	**$ 25,000**
FIXED ASSETS		**LONG TERM DEBT**	
Building	$ 100,000	Mortgage	$ 75,000
Total Fixed Assets	**$ 100,000**	Total Long Term Debt	$ 75,000
		Net Worth	**$ 100,000**
Total	**$ 200,000**	**Total**	**$ 200,000**

(Note the addition of two new accounts: one called long term debt—because it is to be paid over a period longer than one year, and a second account called fixed assets which includes property, plant and equipment.)

When sales are made, inventory will decrease and cash will increase. If some of the sales are made on credit, a new account called Accounts Receivable will need to be added under current assets. Remember, accounts receivable represents cash owed to a business at some future time. It is a current asset because the money

Balance Sheet (CONTINUED)

will normally be paid within one year. Let's suppose that $20,000 of inventory is sold for $25,000. ($15,000 is paid in cash and $10,000 is on credit.) The balance sheet would now look like this:

BALANCE SHEET	XXX COMPANY	YEAR END DATE	
CURRENT ASSETS		**CURRENT LIABILITIES**	
Cash	$ 65,000		
Accounts receivable	$ 10,000	Accounts payable	$ 25,000
Inventory	$ 30,000		
Total Current Assets	**$ 105,000**	**Total Current Liabilities**	**$ 25,000**
FIXED ASSETS		**LONG TERM DEBT**	
Building	$ 100,000	Mortgage	$ 75,000
Total Fixed Assets	**$ 100,000**	**Total Long Term Debt**	**$ 75,000**
		Net Worth Beginning	$ 100,000
		Gross Profit*	$ 5,000
		Net Worth Ending	**$ 105,000**
		Total Liabilities	
Total Assets	**$ 205,000**	**& Net Worth**	**$ 205,000**

(*profit from example sale)

Note that this business action affected three accounts which are on the asset side of the balance sheet, one account, Inventory, decreased because product was sold, Cash increased because the business received cash for part of the sale, Accounts receivable was added/increased because part of the product was sold on credit.

Current assets are listed on the balance sheet in the order of when the account will be converted to cash. For example, accounts receivable is listed before inventory because the business expects to be paid cash from credit customers before it expects to sell all its inventory. The same holds true for current liabilities. They are listed in the order of when the business will pay cash for the amount it owes in the account.

To complete the balance sheet, the company name has been added to the top of the sheet along with the date. The balance sheet shows a company's health or how it stands at a particular point in time.

Glossary of Balance Sheet Terms

Following are the definitions of the terms used in the balance sheet.

Assets	The cash, merchandise, land, buildings and equipment that a company owns or that has a monetary value.
Current Assets	The sum of cash, notes and accounts receivable (less reserves for bad debts), inventories and any other item that can be converted into cash in a short time, usually less than one year.
Cash	Money you have control of and access to.
Accounts Receivable	The monies owed to a company for merchandise, products or services sold or performed but not yet collected.
Inventory	For a manufacturing firm it is the sum of finished merchandise on hand, raw materials and material in process. For retailers and wholesalers, it is the stock of salable goods on hand.
Fixed Assets	Land, buildings, building equipment, fixtures, machinery, tools, furniture, office devices, patterns, drawings, less accumulated depreciation.
Depreciation	A procedure used in accounting to allocate the cost of a fixed asset over that asset's useful life.
Liabilities	Everything that a company owes a creditor; liabilities are the debts owed by the company to others. Liabilities are accounts such as: notes payable, accounts payable or accruals. There are two categories of liabilities, current liabilities and long term liabilities, or as used in this book, long term debt.
Current Liabilities	The total of monies owed by the company that are due within one year.
Short Term Debt	Sometimes called notes payable, money borrowed by the company that will be paid back within one year.

Glossary of Balance Sheet Terms (CONTINUED)

Accounts Payable
Sometimes called trade payable, these are the total of all monies owed by the company to a supplier for all goods and services received but not yet paid for. These goods and services include rent, utilities, office supplies and materials that are used to make goods for sale or are to be resold as they were received.

Accruals
Expenses that are accumulated against current profits but have not yet been paid for in cash.

Mortgage
Legal paper that pledges property to cover a debt.

Long Term Debt
Sometimes called long term liabilities, it is all the obligations such as mortgages, bonds, term loans and any other monies that come due more than one year from the date of the statement.

Net Worth (Owners'/Stockholders' Equity)
What is represented on the balance sheet as the difference between assets and liabilities. In other words, what is due the owners/stockholders of a company.

Common Stock
Money paid to the company by investors to own a piece of the company.

Retained Earnings
Income/profit left in the company from the company's creation less any amount paid out to owners as dividends/withdrawals.

SAMPLE BALANCE SHEETS

The following balance is representative of a sole proprietorship:

XYZ HARDWARE AND BUILDING SUPPLY DECEMBER 31, YEAR BALANCE SHEET			
ASSETS		**LIABILITIES & NET WORTH**	
Cash	$ 2,000	Accounts Payable	$ 18,000
Accounts receivable	85,000	Notes Payable	65,000
Inventory	210,000	Accruals	95,000
Total Current Assets	**$ 297,000**	**Total Current Liabilities**	**$ 178,000**
Land/Buildings	50,000	Mortgage	144,000
Equipment	50,000	Total Long Term Debt	$ 144,000
Furniture & Fixtures	25,000	**Total Liabilities**	**$ 322,000**
Total Fixed Assets	**$ 125,000**		
		Net Worth	**$ 100,000**
Total Assets	**$ 422,000**	**Total Liabilities** **& Net Worth**	**$ 422,000**

The balance sheet on this page is representative of a corporation. Notice the difference in the section which details net worth/stockholders' equity:

XYZ HARDWARE AND BUILDING SUPPLY CORPORATION DECEMBER 31, YEAR BALANCE SHEET			
ASSETS		**LIABILITIES & STOCKHOLDERS' EQUITY**	
Current Assets		Current Liabilities	
Cash	$ 2,000	Accounts Payable	$ 18,000
Accounts Receivable	85,000	Notes Payable	65,000
Inventory	210,000	Accruals	95,000
Total Current Assets	**$ 297,000**	**Total Current Liabilities**	**$ 178,000**
Land/Buildings	50,000		
Equipment	50,000	Mortgage	144,000
Furniture & Fixtures	25,000	**Total Long Term Debt**	**$ 144,000**
Total Fixed Assets	**$ 125,000**		
		Total Liabilities	**$ 322,000**
		Stockholders' Equity	
		Common Stock	57,000
		Retained Earnings	43,000
		Total Stockholders' Equity	**$ 100,000**
Total Assets	**$ 422,000**	**Total Liabilities & Stockholders' Equity**	**$ 422,000**

Why Net Worth Is Not Always the Same as Market Value

A fundamental principle of finance is that all business transactions are recorded on the balance sheet at the dollar value actually agreed upon at the time of the transaction. For example, in the prior balance sheet, the business owner purchased a building for $100,000. That is the dollar amount that appears on the company's balance sheet under the Buildings account regardless of how the building was financed (all cash versus long term debt) and regardless of what the building is appraised at or worth today.

Recording all business transactions at their historic cost is a fundamental accounting principle. For this reason, the net worth of a company shown on the balance sheet should not be confused with the sales or appraised value. Net worth or stockholders' equity on the balance sheet merely reflects the difference between assets and liabilities or what a company owns less what they owe.

The Income Statement

The income statement, often called the profit and loss statement, P&L or statement of operations, shows the performance of a business *over a period of time* be it a month, a quarter or a year. The basic formula for determining performance is:

Revenues - Expenses = Income

The income statement always begins with sales. This is how $25,000 in sales would look on the income statement:

INCOME STATEMENT	
Sales	$25,000

The next item is cost of goods sold. **Cost of goods sold** is normally the manufacturing cost or purchase price of the goods, freight from the supplier, royalties, etc. Cost of goods is subtracted from sales to show gross profit. Let's assume that the cost of the goods sold for the $25,000 shown above was $20,000. Subtracting cost of goods from sales gives a gross profit of $5,000. **Gross profit**, sometimes called *gross margin*, is the amount left over before deducting operating expenses and taxes. The added items would appear on the income statement as shown below:

INCOME STATEMENT	
Sales	$25,000
Cost of Goods Sold	$20,000
Gross Profit	**$ 5,000**

The next entries that go on an income statement are the expenses connected with running the business and are usually referred to as operating expenses. They include such items as rent, utilities, office supplies and overhead. **Operating expenses** can be both cash and accrued. When they are subtracted from gross profit, you are left with **operating income**.

Sometimes businesses have sources of income which are not part of the principal business such as interest income from a bank account. When this is the case, it is considered **other income** and is listed separately after operating income. Income taxes are normally listed separately on the income statement. The words *income*, *profit* and *earnings* are often used synonymously on income statements.

In the following example, expenses totaling $184,200 are identified. Notice that the sample income statement has a heading which shows the company name and that it covers a period of time, in this case a year.

Sample Income Statement

XXX COMPANY JANUARY 1 THROUGH DECEMBER 31 YEAR ANNUAL INCOME STATEMENT		
Sales		$ 700,000
Cost of Goods Sold		500,000
Gross Profit		**200,000**
Expenses		
Salaries*	$ 130,000	
Freight	7,000	
Bad Debt	4,000	
Utilities	7,000	
Depreciation	4,000	
Insurance	7,000	
Taxes (local)	8,000	
Advertising	3,000	
Interest	10,000	
Miscellaneous	4,200	
Total Expenses		**$ 184,200**
Operating Income		$ 15,800
Other Income		$ 500
Income Before Taxes		$ 16,300
Income Taxes		5,400
Net Income		**$ 10,900**

* For the purposes of this book, distributions to owners are considered part of salary expense.

Glossary of Income Statement Terms

Following are the definitions of the terms used in the income statements.

Net Sales	The total dollar volume of all cash or credit sales less returns, allowances, discounts and rebates.
Cost of Goods Sold	For a retail or wholesale business it is the total price paid for the products sold plus the cost of having them delivered to the store during the accounting period.
	For a manufacturing firm, it is the beginning inventory plus purchases, delivery costs, material, labor and overhead less the ending inventory.
Gross Profit	Profit before operating expenses and federal taxes have been deducted.
Operating Expenses	The selling, general and administrative/overhead expenses to run the business. Excludes cost of goods sold, interest and income tax expense. Examples of these costs are rent, utilities, administrative departments such as accounting, marketing, human resources, etc.
Operating Income	The amount left over after subtracting operating expenses from gross profit.
Income Before Taxes	Operating income plus other income.
Net Income	Income before taxes minus income taxes. This is what the business earned in the period. It is added to the balance sheet and increases net worth. Often called net profit or net earnings.

Why Income Does Not Always Equal Cash

With the accrual method of accounting, sales are recorded on the income statement when the goods and/or services associated with those sales are delivered or shipped to a customer. The cost of goods sold are recorded on the income statement *at the same time* the sales are recorded. Sales and cost of goods sold are recorded regardless of when the business receives cash for the goods delivered or when the business had to pay cash for the expense associated with cost of goods sold.

Let's try an example: A hardware store owner orders two electric lawn mowers for sale. The lawnmowers are delivered in March and the owner must pay for them ($100 plus $10 delivery for each mower) in April. He sells one mower to Mr. Jones in March for $180; Mr. Jones pays by check. The other mower doesn't sell until June to a credit customer who does not have to pay until July. What is the effect on the hardware store's cash and income?

	March	April	May	June	July	Total
Cash						
In	$180				$180	$360
Out		($220)				($220)
Net	$180	($220)			$180	$140
Income						
Sales	$180			$180		$360
Cost of Goods Sold	($110)			($110)		($220)
Gross Profit	$70			$70		$140

Even though total cash taken in equals total sales, and total cash paid out equals cost of goods sold, there is a difference in the *timing* of when cash and income are recognized. It is incredibly important for all employees and managers to understand this timing difference. Even though a business may show a profit on the income statement, it cannot continue as a business unless it has the cash flow necessary to pay its bills. Cash is the lifeblood of every business.

The Cash Flow Statement

The previous example explained the difference between income and cash. In any business, a lack of cash, even for a short time, can force a business to close. A cash shortage is very difficult for a business to overcome. Even though a business shows a profit on the income statement, it might not have enough cash to pay its bills. To foresee and hopefully avoid cash flow problems, it is good practice to maintain a cash flow statement.

The balance sheet shows the health of a business as of a specific date. An income statement tells how a business performed over a period of time. Instead of looking back, we will use the cash flow statement as a *planning tool* to help us in the future. This statement will help you target when cash will be needed to pay bills and help managers to make business decisions such as when to expand a business or take on a new product line. The cash flow statement only deals with cash activity—cash paid out and cash taken in. It helps identify those periods when borrowing should be considered. It allows you to make arrangements *before* cash is actually needed. Pre-planning is very helpful when working with bankers.

An estimated cash flow statement should be made during the budgeting process for the year of operations. The year can be broken down by quarter or month to provide greater control. A sample statement appears on the next page. Be sure to include as many line items on your cash flow statement as necessary to make the report useful for you.

Sample Cash Flow Statement

	Forecast Annual Budget	Forecast January	February
Cash In (Sources)			
Beginning Cash Balance	0	0	39,000
Cash Sales	15,000	0	0
Interest Received	50	0	0
Contributions from Owners	60,000	60,000	0
Loans/Borrowed Money	5,000	0	0
Total Receipts	**80,050**	**60,000**	**0**
Cash Out (uses)			
Inventory	7,000	0	0
Operating Expenses	15,000	1,000	1,200
Furniture and Fixtures	20,000	5,000	4,500
Equipment	35,000	15,000	6,500
Income Taxes	1,000	0	0
Distributions to Owners	0	0	0
Total Disbursements	**78,000**	**21,000**	**12,200**
Ending Balance	**2,050**	**39,000**	**26,800**

Glossary of Cash Flow Statement Terms

Cash Sales Cash received from customers for goods and/or services sold. If customers pay on credit, cash would be received when the customers pay their invoice(reduction of accounts receivables).

Interest Received Money received from cash invested in money market accounts, certificates of deposit and/or other short term highly liquid investments.

Contributions/Investment Cash given to a business in exchange for an ownership interest. Could be cash from the sale of company stock.

Loans/Borrowed Money Money received from bankers/investors from the issuance of company notes/debt.

Inventory Money used to purchase items held for sale or used in the manufacture of products that will be sold.

Operating Expenses Cash used to pay salaries, rent, supplies, utilities, administration, etc. necessary for the day-to-day operations of the business.

Furniture and Fixtures Money spent to acquire furniture and fixtures (fixed assets) required to run or expand the business.

Equipment Money spent to acquire equipment (fixed assets) required to run or expand the business.

Income Taxes Money paid to the federal, state or local taxing authority that is based on income.

Distribution to Owners Money paid to owners/investors as a cash return on their investment in the company.

Summary of Part 1

Congratulations! You now understand the basic financial statements common to all businesses. These tools are only the beginning of financial analysis. The balance sheet and income statement alone do not provide sufficient information to properly operate a business. For instance, these documents alone cannot tell you the answers to the following questions:

➤ Can a business pay its bills?

➤ Is a business becoming more or less profitable?

➤ Can the business borrow money? Does it need to?

➤ Is the company a good investment for stockholders?

The answers to these and other key questions come from knowing how to use the information in a balance sheet and income statement.

Basic financial information can be used to develop simple ratios that will help you understand and control a business. Looking at your expenses as percents of sales can help you reduce your costs. Keeping track of selected ratios and percentages over a period of time will help you chart the future with confidence. This is what you are about to learn in the pages ahead.

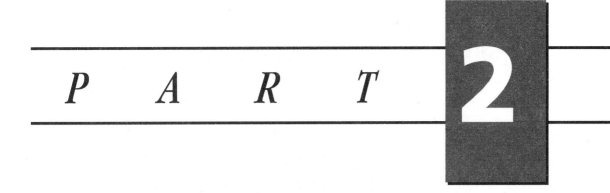

P A R T 2

Understanding
Ratios and
Percentages

Using Ratios Without Fear

Think of a ratio as a friend when scrutinizing your business. Ratios are simple to calculate, especially with a hand held calculator, and easy to use. They provide a wealth of information that cannot be obtained anywhere else.

Ratios cannot take the place of experience or replace good management, but they will make good managers better. Ratios can help to point out areas that need more investigation or assist in developing future operating strategy.

You can quickly learn to use a number of ratios by following the steps outlined in the book. The "fill-in-the-blank" forms presented later will assist you in analyzing any business. Going through the forms provided should allow you to understand basic ratios and be comfortable using them.

Stay with this part. It is important. It may sound complex at first, but will become clearer as you use ratios.

Why Ratio Analysis?

Ratios are common. You use them every day. They provide a better understanding of a wide range of situations. For instance, the miles you get per gallon of gasoline or the unemployment rate presented as a ratio are easier to grasp than the total number of gallons of gas used or the total number of unemployed people. Ratios are used when we look for the best price per ounce for food, when we compare batting averages of baseball players or we measure the cost of building in dollars per square foot.

Ratios are an even more important tool to measure the progress of a business and to compare a business to its competitors.

How Ratios Are Developed

Ratios are expressed by placing one number over another number. For example:

$$\frac{50}{100}$$

is a ratio. It means that 50 is to be divided by 100. The answer will be a percentage. In this case, .50 or 50% because 50 is one half of 100.

The number on top of a formula represents the figure you are comparing to the bottom figure (which is called the base). For instance, if the 50 in the above ratio represents 50 dollars in sales and 100 represents 100 dollars of fixed assets (such as a piece of equipment or fixture), you are able to compare the amount of sales generated by the fixed assets, or 50%.

Another way to express this is to use proportions. This means that sales to fixed assets is in the proportion of 1 to 2.

If the numbers were reversed: $\frac{100}{50}$

then sales become 100 dollars and fixed assets 50 dollars. In this case, the fixed assets generated 200% or 2 times their value. In other words, 50 can go into 100 twice. The proportion of fixed assets to sales is now 1 to 2. Ratios are used to indicate how a business is doing. They do not make decisions for you in themselves, but do provide information from which to make sound decisions. More than one ratio should be examined before a major decision is made, but more on this later. Right now, let's dig deeper into percentages and ratios.

What Ratios Measure

Ratios measure proportions. In our example of $\frac{100}{50}$ above, we were able to determine what proportion one figure is of another. Ratios also measure relationships. They do this because they can translate assets, such as tools and inventory, and liabilities, such as payables and loans, into common dollar figures. By doing this, it is easy to see valuable relationships between two seemingly unrelated items. Ratios also allow you to make comparisons between time periods. For example, a ratio lets you measure your inventory turnover from one month to another, or year to year.

How Ratios Are Developed (CONTINUED)

Trend Analysis

By calculating the same percentages or ratios at the same time each month or year, you can look for trends in a business. Trends illustrate the extent and direction of change over time. Generally, trend analysis is performed at the end of each month.

The 10% Paradox

Suppose you are asked if you would be willing to take a chance on an event that would pay you $100,000. All you had to do was call "heads or tails" at the fair flip of a coin. Probability laws tell you that you have a 50 - 50 chance of winning. But suppose you have to risk $10,000 (10%) to participate in the coin flip? You might shy away from putting $10,000 at risk even though the payoff was large. However, you might be willing to risk less to get less, i.e. 10% of $1,000 or $100. In other words, even though the percentage did not change, spending a large amount of "real" money would make the difference. Ratios and percentages, therefore, need to be kept in context as to what they represent.

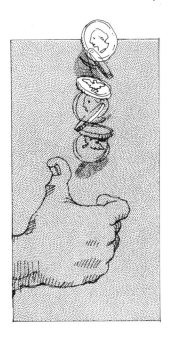

Five Basic Rules for Ratios

To ease you into the use of ratios, carefully review the following five basic rules:

1. To determine a percentage change, always make sure you know what your base is. For example, suppose your sales increased 25% the first month of the year and 37% the second month. It would be wrong to state the second month's increase was 12%. This is because both were taken from the same base period (in this case 100). The second month showed 12 percentage points increase. To determine the actual monthly increase, the 12 point increase of the second month should be divided by the new base period of 125 (the beginning figure, 100, plus the first month's increase of 25) for a true monthly increase of 9.6% (12/125 = .096 or 9.6%) in the second month.

2. When comparing a part to a whole, such as net profits to sales, the whole is always the base. That is: $\dfrac{\text{net profits}}{\text{sales}}$

3. A percent of something can increase by more than 100% but cannot decrease by more than 100%. Think of it like this: you can double your money, 200%, but you can lose only 100% of it.

4. Ratios lose significance and accuracy when they become excessively detailed. This is important because it means that you don't need a lot of detailed data or figures to use ratio analysis. Analysis is often significant when used in general ways, i.e., "ballpark" figures.

5. Remember that ratios will assist you in decision making not make decisions for you.

Cautions to Keep in Mind When Using Ratios

Maintain An Objective Attitude. Don't use ratios to support predetermined conclusions. Use them to help you better understand your business.

Don't Use The Wrong Figures. For instance, when looking at a percent change between two dollar figures, such as a raise in price from $2.00 to $3.00, the number you want to compare is the difference between the two dollar figures which is $1.00. This difference figure ($1.00) is then divided by $2.00 for a percent raise of 50%. Don't divide $2.00 by $3.00 or vice versa.

Don't Compare Meaningless Numbers. For example, don't compare expenses to fixed assets. This number is easy to calculate but has no meaning in the operation of a business.

Summary of Part 2

➤ You have been introduced to ratio analysis and now know that ratios are expressed as a percent or a proportion.

➤ You discovered that ratios are developed by dividing the number you wish to compare by the base number.

➤ You learned that by taking these ratio measurements regularly (monthly, quarterly, annually) you can see trends that can be an early warning signal or a green light to go forward.

➤ You have regularly used ratios in many home and business transactions. These are developed the same way as the ratios we will learn to use in this book.

➤ You learned that ratios are expressed like this:

$$\frac{50}{100} = 50\% \text{ or } 1 \text{ to } 2 \text{ (1:2)}$$

and

$$\frac{100}{50} = 200\% \text{ or } 2 \text{ to } 1 \text{ (2:1)}$$

➤ You discovered that ratios can be easy to develop and use and noted a few basic rules and cautions that will enable you to understand them better.

➤ Finally, we hope you know that ratios are friends and can help you control your business.

HINT:

If the top number in a ratio is smaller than the bottom number, the ratio will be a percent less than 100%. If the top number is larger than the bottom number, the ratio will be greater than 100%.

Four Types
of Ratios

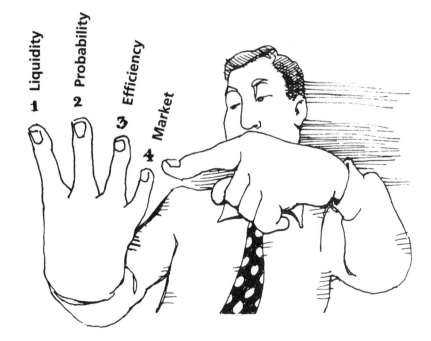

Introduction to Ratios

This part of the book presents and explains several common ratios that can be used to measure and control a business. You will not use every ratio that is presented, especially if you are in a service business. It is not necessary to memorize the ratios or their meanings presented in this part because you can always return to this part of the book for reference.

The first set of ratios are called **liquidity ratios** because they measure the amount of cash available to cover expenses both current and long term. These ratios are especially important in keeping a business alive. Not paying your bills due to a shortage of cash is the fastest way to go out of business. Lending institutions often don't want to loan money when it is actually needed the most. Make arrangements ahead of time for a line-of-credit. The best time to do this is when your business liquidity looks very good. (Make sure your line-of-credit agreement is always in writing!)

The second set of ratios is called **profitability ratios**. These ratios measure and help control income. This is done through higher sales, larger margins, getting more from your expenses and/or a combination of these methods.

The third set of ratios is called **efficiency ratios**. Efficiency ratios measure and help control the operation of the business. They add another dimension to help you increase income by assessing such important transactions as the use of credit, control of inventory and/or management of assets.

The fourth set of ratios is called **market ratios**. Market ratios are primarily used by investors to determine whether or not to purchase stock in a company. Several market ratios are reported on the stock pages of most daily newspapers. Although these ratios may not be important to many small businesses, it is important to know what they are and how to calculate them.

How to Use This Section

An explanation of each ratio is presented on a left page, illustrated by a balance sheet and profit and loss statement on the facing page. Each figure used to develop a ratio is highlighted on these statements using a shaded area.

Glossary for Ratio Analysis

Current Assets The sum of cash, notes and accounts receivable (less reserves for bad debts), inventories and any other item that can be converted into cash in a short time, usually less than one year.

Current Liabilities The total of monies owed by the company that are due within one year.

Net Sales The total dollar volume of all cash or credit sales less returns, allowances, discounts and rebates.

Working Capital Current assets less current liabilities.

Net Worth (Owners'/Stockholders' Equity)–What is represented on the balance sheet as the difference between assets and liabilities. In other words, what is due the owners/stockholders of a company.

Income Before Taxes Operating income plus other income before income taxes.

Net Income Income before taxes minus income taxes. This is what the business earned in the period. It is added to the balance sheet and increases net worth. Often called net profit or net earnings.

Total Assets The sum of all current and fixed/long term assets.

Accounts Receivable The monies owed to a company for merchandise, products or services sold or performed but not yet collected.

Cost of Goods Sold For a retail or wholesale business it is the total price paid for the products sold plus the cost of having them delivered to the store during the accounting period.

Inventory For a manufacturing firm it is the sum of finished merchandise on hand, raw materials and material in process. For retailers and wholesalers, it is the stock of salable goods on hand.

Fixed Assets Land, buildings, building equipment, fixtures, machinery, tools, furniture, office devices, patterns, drawings, less accumulated depreciation.

Ratio 1: Liquidity Ratios

Current Ratio

Measures:
The ability to meet short term obligations.

Generally Accepted Standard:
Current assets should be 2 times or 200% of current liabilities.

Low Ratio:
A company may not be able to pay off bills as rapidly as it should. It may not be able to take advantage of cash discounts or other favorable terms. It may not be able to keep its suppliers happy and receive good service. High inventory means high accounts payable.

High Ratio:
Money that could be working for the business is tied up in government securities, cash savings or other safe funds.

Remarks:
The proper ratio for a business depends on the type of business, the time in the business cycle and the age of the business. You need to inquire about what is customary in your type of business.

Quick Ratio:
Another variation is the quick ratio (or acid test) which is the same as the current ratio except that it eliminates inventory so that only cash and accounts receivable assets are counted. Some analysts reduce accounts receivable by 25% before using this ratio. Whether you do or not depends on how much faith you have in your ability to collect your debts. The ratio looks like this:

$$\frac{\text{cash} + \text{accounts receivable}}{\text{current liabilities}} = \frac{2,000 + 85,000}{178,000} = .49\text{:}1 \text{ or } .49 \text{ Times or } 49\%$$

The quick ratio measures your immediate liquidity or the cash you have to cover your immediate liabilities. A safe margin would be at least 100% or 1.0 times. The example above is less than one-half to one and suggests some serious problems such as slow moving inventory.

XYZ HARDWARE AND BUILDING SUPPLY BALANCE SHEET
DECEMBER 31, YEAR

ASSETS		LIABILITIES	
Current Assets		Current Liabilities	
Cash	$ 2,000	Accounts Payable	$ 18,000
Accounts Receivable	85,000	Notes Payable	65,000
Inventory	210,000	Accruals	95,000
Total Current Assets	**$ 297,000**	**Total Current Liabilities**	**$ 178,000**
Fixed Assets		Long Term Liabilities	
Land	$ 50,000	Long Term Debt	$ 144,000
Equipment	50,000	**Total Liabilities**	**$ 322,000**
Furniture & Fixtures	25,000		
Total Fixed Assets	**$ 125,000**	Net Worth	$ 100,000
Total Assets	**$ 422,000**	**Total Liabilities and Net Worth**	**$ 422,000**

XYZ HARDWARE AND BUILDING SUPPLY INCOME STATEMENT
FOR YEAR ENDING DECEMBER 31, YEAR

Net Sales (less allowances)		$ 700,000
Cost of Goods Sold		500,000
Gross (Margin) Profit		**$ 200,000**
Expenses		
Salaries	$ 130,000	
Freight	7,000	
Bad Debt	4,000	
Utilities	7,000	
Depreciation	4,000	
Insurance	7,000	
Taxes (local)	8,000	
Advertising	3,000	
Interest	10,000	
Miscellaneous	4,200	
Total Operating Expenses		**$ 184,200**
Operating Income		$ 15,800
Other Income		500
Income Before Taxes		**$ 16,300**

Current Ratio

$$\frac{\text{Current Assets}}{\text{Current Liabilities}} = \frac{\$297,000}{\$178,000} = 1.7:1 \text{ or } 1.7 \text{ Times}$$

Liquidity Ratios (CONTINUED)

Turnover of Cash Ratio

Measures:

The turnover of cash or working capital. Maintaining a positive cash flow or working capital balance will provide an adequate means to finance your sales without struggling to pay for the material and/or goods you are buying.

Generally Accepted Standard:

Sales should be 5 or 6 times working capital.

Low Ratio:

You may have funds tied up in short-term low-yielding assets. This means that you may get by on less cash.

High Ratio:

A vulnerability to creditors, such as the inability to pay wages or utility bills.

Remarks:

Usually, if the current ratio (current assets/current liabilities) ratio is low, the turnover of cash ratio will be high. This is due to the small amount of working capital that is available.

NOTE:

It's called working capital because it is the amount necessary to operate your business on a daily basis. Working capital is the money you use for salaries, to pay your bills, etc. The amount of your working capital changes every time you receive cash, make a cash sale or write a check.

XYZ HARDWARE AND BUILDING SUPPLY BALANCE SHEET
DECEMBER 31, YEAR

ASSETS		LIABILITIES	
Current Assets		Current Liabilities	
Cash	$ 2,000	Accounts Payable	$ 18,000
Accounts Receivable	85,000	Notes Payable	65,000
Inventory	210,000	Accruals	95,000
Total Current Assets	**$ 297,000**	**Total Current Liabilities**	**$ 178,000**
Fixed Assets		Long Term Liabilities	
Land	$ 50,000	Long Term Debt	$ 144,000
Equipment	50,000	**Total Liabilities**	**$ 322,000**
Furniture & Fixtures	25,000		
Total Fixed Assets	**$ 125,000**	Net Worth	$ 100,000
Total Assets	**$ 422,000**	**Total Liabilities**	
		and Net Worth	**$ 422,000**

XYZ HARDWARE AND BUILDING SUPPLY INCOME STATEMENT
FOR YEAR ENDING DECEMBER 31, YEAR

Net Sales (less allowances)		$ 700,000
Cost of Goods Sold		500,000
Gross (Margin) Profit		**$ 200,000**
Expenses		
Salaries	$ 130,000	
Freight	7,000	
Bad Debt	4,000	
Utilities	7,000	
Depreciation	4,000	
Insurance	7,000	
Taxes (local)	8,000	
Advertising	3,000	
Interest	10,000	
Miscellaneous	4,200	
Total Operating Expenses		**$ 184,200**
Operating Income		$ 15,800
Other Income		500
Income Before Taxes		**$ 16,300**

Turnover of Cash Ratio

$$\frac{\text{Net Sales}}{\text{Working Capital*}} = \frac{\$700,000}{\$119,000} = 5.9:1 \text{ or } 5.9 \text{ Times}$$

*(Working Capital = Current Assets - Current Liabilities = $297,000 - 178,000 = $119,000)

Liquidity Ratios (CONTINUED)

Debt to Equity Ratio

Measures:
Debt ratio expresses the relationship between capital contributed by the creditors (suppliers and banks) that loan a business cash and owners equity remaining in the business.

Generally Accepted Standard:
Some analysts feel that current liabilities to net worth should not exceed 80% and long term debt should not exceed net worth by 50% or creditors might want to have a say in how the business is operated or an ownership interest.

Low Ratio:
Greater long term financial safety. This would generally mean you have greater flexibility to borrow money. An extremely low ratio may mean that the firm's management is too fiscally conservative. This may indicate the firm is not reaching its full profit potential, that is, the profit potential from leverage, which is realized by borrowing money at a low rate of interest and obtaining a higher rate of return on sales.

High Ratio:
Greater risk being assumed by the creditors, hence greater interest by them in the way the firm is being managed. Your ability to obtain money from outside sources is limited.

Remarks:
Again, a lot depends on where business is in its life cycle, what the policies of the owners are, the state of the economy and the particular business cycle. Remember long term debt is leverage. Leverage can work for you during the good time and work against you during a sales slump. This can create decreased earnings if too much money is borrowed.

XYZ HARDWARE AND BUILDING SUPPLY BALANCE SHEET
DECEMBER 31, YEAR

ASSETS		LIABILITIES	
Current Assets		Current Liabilities	
Cash	$ 2,000	Accounts Payable	$ 18,000
Accounts Receivable	85,000	Notes Payable	65,000
Inventory	210,000	Accruals	95,000
Total Current Assets	**$ 297,000**	**Total Current Liabilities**	**$ 178,000**
Fixed Assets		Long Term Liabilities	
Land	$ 50,000	Long Term Debt	$ 144,000
Equipment	50,000	**Total Liabilities**	**$ 322,000**
Furniture & Fixtures	25,000	Net Worth	$ 100,000
Total Fixed Assets	**$ 125,000**	**Total Liabilities**	
Total Assets	**$ 422,000**	**and Net Worth**	**$ 422,000**

XYZ HARDWARE AND BUILDING SUPPLY INCOME STATEMENT
FOR YEAR ENDING DECEMBER 31, YEAR

Net Sales (less allowances)		$ 700,000
Cost of Goods Sold		500,000
Gross (Margin) Profit		**$ 200,000**
Expenses		
Salaries	$ 130,000	
Freight	7,000	
Bad Debt	4,000	
Utilities	7,000	
Depreciation	4,000	
Insurance	7,000	
Taxes (local)	8,000	
Advertising	3,000	
Interest	10,000	
Miscellaneous	4,200	
Total Operating Expenses		**$ 184,200**
Operating Income		$ 15,800
Other Income		500
Income Before Taxes		**$ 16,300**

Debt to Equity Ratio

$$\frac{\text{Total Debt*}}{\text{Equity**}} = \frac{\$322,000}{\$100,000} = 3.2{:}1 \text{ or } 3.2 \text{ Times or } 322\%$$

* (Total Debt = Total Liabilities)

** (Equity = Net Worth = Total Assets - Total Liabilities = $422,000 - 322,000 = $100,000)

Summary of Liquidity Ratios

Having read this far you are well on your way to mastering the use of ratio analysis.

➤ Liquidity ratios help you determine your firm's ability to pay debts.

➤ The current ratio is important as it provides an indication of your ability to pay your immediate bills.

➤ Working capital is the difference between current assets and current liabilities. This is an important figure because it represents the amount available to pay for salaries or new material or goods.

➤ By maintaining a proper ratio for your turnover of cash, you will be able to take advantage of discounts for prompt payment.

➤ Your total long term debt should not exceed 45% of your net worth.

Ratio 2: Profitability Ratios

Profitability is why most of us are in business. We want a better return on our money and time than we can get from a bank or other low-risk interest-paying opportunity. This, by the way, is one of the most commonly used methods to evaluate whether you are doing well with your business. For example, if savings accounts or money market accounts are paying a higher percent than you are earning on the money you have invested in a business, you will probably want to consider selling your business investment and reinvesting your money elsewhere unless you particularly like your business investment better than making more money. Profitability ratios provide you with the means to measure your earnings in several ways (as we will soon see). They measure your return on sales, return on assets and return on investment.

As a general rule, profitability, or income as it is sometimes called, comes about from changes in price or volume or both. Therefore, changes in your ratios over time will come about by what you do that affects changes in your price and/or volume. This will be noted by increases in expenses such as for more salespeople or advertising, changes will take place over time as assets are depreciated or new ones are added, or if borrowing takes place. If you raise or lower your prices, changes will usually be shown by changes in your ratios.

Profitability Ratios (CONTINUED)

Rate of Return on Sales Ratio

Measures:
How much operating income, sometimes called net profit, was derived from every dollar of sales. It indicates how well you have managed your operating expenses. It may also indicate whether the business is generating enough sales to cover the fixed costs and still leave an acceptable profit.

Generally Accepted Standard:
Depends on the business and/or the industry. Price and volume are important and play a large role in determining this ratio.

Low Ratio:
May not mean too much in some industries; for instance, a business that has a high turnover of inventory or one that uses low margin to attract business such as a grocery store might show a low ratio but still be healthy.

High Ratio:
Usually the higher the ratio the better. However, if you are beating last year's figures and show steady increase, you are on the right track.

Remarks:
In analyzing your business, this ratio must be viewed with many facts in mind and used in conjunction with other ratios and analytical tools. Beware of using this ratio alone as you can easily begin comparing apples with oranges. Comparing it with your own results month after month or year after year is valid. This is an application of trend analysis.

XYZ HARDWARE AND BUILDING SUPPLY BALANCE SHEET
DECEMBER 31, YEAR

ASSETS		LIABILITIES	
Current Assets		Current Liabilities	
Cash	$ 2,000	Accounts Payable	$ 18,000
Accounts Receivable	85,000	Notes Payable	65,000
Inventory	210,000	Accruals	95,000
Total Current Assets	**$ 297,000**	**Total Current Liabilities**	**$ 178,000**
Fixed Assets		Long Term Liabilities	
Land	$ 50,000	Long Term Debt	$ 144,000
Equipment	50,000	**Total Liabilities**	**$ 322,000**
Furniture & Fixtures	25,000	Net Worth	$ 100,000
Total Fixed Assets	**$ 125,000**	**Total Liabilities**	
Total Assets	**$ 422,000**	**and Net Worth**	**$ 422,000**

XYZ HARDWARE AND BUILDING SUPPLY INCOME STATEMENT
FOR YEAR ENDING DECEMBER 31, YEAR

Net Sales (less allowances)		$ 700,000
Cost of Goods Sold		500,000
Gross (Margin) Profit		**$ 200,000**
Expenses		
Salaries	$ 130,000	
Freight	7,000	
Bad Debt	4,000	
Utilities	7,000	
Depreciation	4,000	
Insurance	7,000	
Taxes (local)	8,000	
Advertising	3,000	
Interest	10,000	
Miscellaneous	4,200	
Total Operating Expenses		**$ 184,200**
Operating Income		$ 15,800
Other Income		500
Income Before Taxes		**$ 16,300**

Rate of Return on Sales Ratio

$$\frac{\text{Operating Income}}{\text{Net Sales}} = \frac{\$15,800}{\$700,000} = 2.3\%$$

Profitability Ratios (CONTINUED)

Rate of Return on Assets Ratio (ROA)

Measures:
The income (profit) that is generated by the use of the assets of the business.

Generally Accepted Standard:
Varies a great deal depending on the industry and the amount of fixed assets required by the business, the amount of cash that must be available, etc. For example, an oil company must have refineries which require an enormous amount of fixed assets, while a men's clothing store would have minimal fixed asset requirements.

Low Ratio:
Poor performance, or ineffective use of the assets by management.

High Ratio:
Good performance, or effective use of the firm's assets by management.

Remarks:
This ratio can easily be distorted by a heavily depreciated plant, a large amount of intangible assets (nonphysical, such as patents) or unusual income or expense items. This ratio should be used with other ratios to compare firms in the same industry and of approximately the same size. It is a valid tool if you know the real value of your competitor's assets (especially fixed assets) and whether they are including outside earnings as a large part of their current assets. If you don't know, beware of making a definite conclusion from this ratio alone.

A variation of this ratio would be to look at current and fixed assets separately and work a ratio on each of them. Knowing the return on fixed assets (ROFA) could be important to a business that has to count on heavy investment in fixed assets such as rolling stock or heavy machinery to generate sales and profits.

XYZ HARDWARE AND BUILDING SUPPLY BALANCE SHEET
DECEMBER 31, YEAR

ASSETS		LIABILITIES	
Current Assets		Current Liabilities	
Cash	$ 2,000	Accounts Payable	$ 18,000
Accounts Receivable	85,000	Notes Payable	65,000
Inventory	210,000	Accruals	95,000
Total Current Assets	**$ 297,000**	**Total Current Liabilities**	**$ 178,000**
Fixed Assets		Long Term Liabilities	
Land	$ 50,000	Long Term Debt	$ 144,000
Equipment	50,000	**Total Liabilities**	**$ 322,000**
Furniture & Fixtures	25,000		
Total Fixed Assets	**$ 125,000**	Net Worth	$ 100,000
Total Assets	**$ 422,000**	**Total Liabilities and Net Worth**	**$ 422,000**

XYZ HARDWARE AND BUILDING SUPPLY INCOME STATEMENT
FOR YEAR ENDING DECEMBER 31, YEAR

Net Sales (less allowances)		$ 700,000
Cost of Goods Sold		500,000
Gross (Margin) Profit		**$ 200,000**
Expenses		
Salaries	$ 130,000	
Freight	7,000	
Bad Debt	4,000	
Utilities	7,000	
Depreciation	4,000	
Insurance	7,000	
Taxes (local)	8,000	
Advertising	3,000	
Interest	10,000	
Miscellaneous	4,200	
Total Operating Expenses		**$ 184,200**
Operating Income		$ 15,800
Other Income		500
Income Before Taxes		**$ 16,300**

Rate of Return on Assets Ratio (ROA)

$$\frac{\text{Income Before Taxes}}{\text{Total Assets}} = \frac{\$16,300}{\$422,000} = 3.9\%$$

Profitability Ratios (CONTINUED)

Rate of Return on Investment Ratio (ROI)

Measures:
Return on the owner's investment (ROI). Some use this figure as a final evaluation to determine whether or not to invest in a company. This ratio is also called return on equity (ROE).

Generally Accepted Standard:
A return on investment of 15% is generally considered necessary to fund future growth from within a business. This means that a business will not be dependent on financing its growth with long term debt, but will be able to generate the income from its own operations.

Low Ratio:
Perhaps you could have done better investing your money else where. This could indicate inefficient management performance or it could reflect a highly capitalized, conservatively operated business with little long term debt.

High Ratio:
Perhaps creditors were a source of much of the funds used in the business, management is efficient or the firm is undercapitalized (has minimal long term debt).

Remarks:
This measure is considered one of the best criteria of profitability; it can be a key ratio to compare against other firms or the industry average. However, it should be used in conjunction with other ratios. There should be a direct relationship between ROI and risk; that is, the greater the risk, the higher the return. Remember, net worth is the difference between assets and liabilities, or equity. A smaller net worth figure would equate to a higher ratio.

Another Measure of ROI is:

$$\frac{\text{EBIT*}}{\text{Net Worth}} = \frac{26,300}{100,000} = 26.3\%$$

*EBIT = earnings before interest and taxes
        = income before taxes + interest
        = \$16,300 + \$10,000
        = \$26,300

XYZ HARDWARE AND BUILDING SUPPLY BALANCE SHEET
DECEMBER 31, YEAR

ASSETS		LIABILITIES	
Current Assets		**Current Liabilities**	
Cash	$ 2,000	Accounts Payable	$ 18,000
Accounts Receivable	85,000	Notes Payable	65,000
Inventory	210,000	Accruals	95,000
Total Current Assets	**$ 297,000**	**Total Current Liabilities**	**$ 178,000**
Fixed Assets		**Long Term Liabilities**	
Land	$ 50,000	Long Term Debt	$ 144,000
Equipment	50,000	**Total Liabilities**	**$ 322,000**
Furniture & Fixtures	25,000	Net Worth	$ 100,000
Total Fixed Assets	**$ 125,000**	**Total Liabilities**	
Total Assets	**$ 422,000**	**and Net Worth**	**$ 422,000**

XYZ HARDWARE AND BUILDING SUPPLY INCOME STATEMENT
FOR YEAR ENDING DECEMBER 31, YEAR

Net Sales (less allowances)		$ 700,000
Cost of Goods Sold		500,000
Gross (Margin) Profit		**$ 200,000**
Expenses		
Salaries	$ 130,000	
Freight	7,000	
Bad Debt	4,000	
Utilities	7,000	
Depreciation	4,000	
Insurance	7,000	
Taxes (local)	8,000	
Advertising	3,000	
Interest	10,000	
Miscellaneous	4,200	
Total Operating Expenses		**$ 184,200**
Operating Income		$ 15,800
Other Income		500
Income Before Taxes		**$ 16,300**

Rate of Return on Investments Ratio (ROI)

$$\frac{\text{Income Before Taxes}}{\text{Net Worth}} = \frac{\$16,300}{\$100,000} = 16.3\%$$

Summary of Profitability Ratios

➤ Profitability ratios measure return on sales, return on assets and return on investment.

➤ Profitability is a result of several things such as: your price structure, the amount of business you do and how well you control your expenses.

➤ Profitability ratios are a valid tool to compare your business to your industry average.

➤ Your return on investment can be compared as a return on net worth to total assets.

➤ The rate of return on sales must be used with caution when comparing your business with that of others.

➤ Beware of using the rate of return on total assets ratio to compare your business with others without knowing: the condition of the fixed assets; if the fixed assets are leased; and if outside earnings are a part of current assets.

Ratio 3: Efficiency Ratios

Efficiency ratios measure how well you are conducting your business. These ratios provide an indication of how fast you are collecting your money for credit sales and how many times you are turning over your inventory in a given period of time. They measure the amount of sales generated by your assets and the return you are earning on your assets.

Efficiency ratios are an important benchmark to keeping your business in balance. For instance, if you become too loose in offering credit to generate sales, this will show up as an increase in the average number of days it takes to collect your accounts receivable. If you over-buy, even with well-meaning intentions of not passing up a real bargain, this will be reflected in a decrease in the turnover of your inventory. Similarly, if you acquire too many fixed assets without a corresponding increase in sales, your fixed asset turnover ratio will quickly decline.

Of course, other ratios will also play a part in maintaining a balance in your business that will aid you in maintaining healthy growth, but the efficiency ratios will usually note it sooner. You will notice that some efficiency ratios are in days and not percentages or proportions.

Efficiency Ratios (CONTINUED)

Average Collection Period Ratio

Measures:
The turnover of receivables is the average number of days it takes to collect cash from your credit sales.

Generally Accepted Standard:
Depends on your collection period policy—if you invoice with balance due in thirty days, then thirty days is the standard.

Low Ratio:
A fast turnover—which could be the result of a stringent collection policy or fast-paying customers.

High Ratio:
A slow turnover—which may be the result of a number of bad accounts, or a tax collection policy or perhaps credit is being used to generate sales.

Remarks:
Generally anything within 10 to 15 days of your collection policy is deemed acceptable and considered within the collection period.

XYZ HARDWARE AND BUILDING SUPPLY BALANCE SHEET
DECEMBER 31, YEAR

ASSETS			LIABILITIES		
Current Assets			Current Liabilities		
Cash	$	2,000	Accounts Payable	$	18,000
Accounts Receivable		85,000	Notes Payable		65,000
Inventory		210,000	Accruals		95,000
Total Current Assets		**$ 297,000**	**Total Current Liabilities**		**$ 178,000**
Fixed Assets			Long Term Liabilities		
Land	$	50,000	Long Term Debt		$ 144,000
Equipment		50,000	**Total Liabilities**		**$ 322,000**
Furniture & Fixtures		25,000			
Total Fixed Assets		**$ 125,000**	Net Worth		$ 100,000
Total Assets		**$ 422,000**	**Total Liabilities and Net Worth**		**$ 422,000**

XYZ HARDWARE AND BUILDING SUPPLY INCOME STATEMENT
FOR YEAR ENDING DECEMBER 31, YEAR

Net Sales (less allowances)		$ 700,000
Cost of Goods Sold		500,000
Gross (Margin) Profit		**$ 200,000**
Expenses		
Salaries	$ 130,000	
Freight	7,000	
Bad Debt	4,000	
Utilities	7,000	
Depreciation	4,000	
Insurance	7,000	
Taxes (local)	8,000	
Advertising	3,000	
Interest	10,000	
Miscellaneous	4,200	
Total Operating Expenses		**$ 184,200**
Operating Income		$ 15,800
Other Income		500
Income Before Taxes		**$ 16,300**

Average Collection Period Ratio

$$\frac{\text{Accounts Receivable* x Days/Year}}{\text{Net Sles}} = \frac{\$85,000 \times 365}{\$700,000} = 44 \text{ Days}$$

* For this calculation, all sales are assumed to be credit sales.

Efficiency Ratios (CONTINUED)

Inventory Turnover Ratio

Measures:
Inventory turnover. This measures how fast your merchandise is moving. That is, how many times your initial inventory is replaced in a year.

Generally Accepted Standard:
Depends on the industry and even the time of year for some industries. However 6 to 7 times is a rule of thumb.

Low Ratio:
An indication of a large inventory, a never-out-of-stock situation, perhaps some obsolete items, or it could indicate poor liquidity, some possible overstocking of items or a planned build-up in anticipation of a coming high-selling period.

High Ratio:
An indication of a narrow selection, maybe fast-moving merchandise, or perhaps some lost sales due to lack of stock. It may indicate better liquidity or even superior merchandising.

Remarks:
Faster turnovers are generally viewed as a positive trend; they increase cash flow and reduce warehousing costs, etc. This ratio measures how management is using inventory and can be used to compare one period to the next or to another company in the same industry or the industry average. Again, it's an indicator, not an absolute measure or count. As a general rule, a small retail business should not carry more than 100% of its working capital (current assets less current liabilities) in inventory.

Note: _____

Average inventory is beginning inventory plus ending inventory divided by 2. For the purpose of our calculation, we used ending inventory to approximate the average.

Manufacturers inventory = finished goods + raw materials + in-process materials
Retailers/wholesalers inventory = salable goods on hand

XYZ HARDWARE AND BUILDING SUPPLY BALANCE SHEET
DECEMBER 31, YEAR

ASSETS			LIABILITIES		
Current Assets			Current Liabilities		
Cash	$	2,000	Accounts Payable	$	18,000
Accounts Receivable		85,000	Notes Payable		65,000
Inventory		210,000	Accruals		95,000
Total Current Assets		**$ 297,000**	**Total Current Liabilities**		**$ 178,000**
Fixed Assets			Long Term Liabilities		
Land	$	50,000	Long Term Debt		$ 144,000
Equipment		50,000	**Total Liabilities**		**$ 322,000**
Furniture & Fixtures		25,000	Net Worth		$ 100,000
Total Fixed Assets		**$ 125,000**	**Total Liabilities**		
Total Assets		**$ 422,000**	**and Net Worth**		**$ 422,000**

XYZ HARDWARE AND BUILDING SUPPLY INCOME STATEMENT
FOR YEAR ENDING DECEMBER 31, YEAR

Net Sales (less allowances)		$ 700,000
Cost of Goods Sold		500,000
Gross (Margin) Profit		**$ 200,000**
Expenses		
Salaries	$ 130,000	
Freight	7,000	
Bad Debt	4,000	
Utilities	7,000	
Depreciation	4,000	
Insurance	7,000	
Taxes (local)	8,000	
Advertising	3,000	
Interest	10,000	
Miscellaneous	4,200	
Total Operating Expenses		**$ 184,200**
Operating Income		$ 15,800
Other Income		500
Income Before Taxes		**$ 16,300**

Inventory Turnover Ratio	**Number of Days in Inventory Ratio**
$\dfrac{\text{Cost of Goods Sold}}{\text{Average Inventory}} = \dfrac{\$500,000}{\$210,000} = 2.4 \text{ times}$	$\dfrac{\text{Days in 1 Year}}{\text{Inventory Turnover}} = \dfrac{365 \text{ Days}}{2.4 \text{ Times}} = \dfrac{152 \text{ Days}}{\text{in inventory}}$

Efficiency Ratios (CONTINUED)

Fixed Asset Turnover Ratio (also called Net Sales to Fixed Assets Ratio)

Measures:
Measures management's effectiveness in generating sales from investments in fixed assets. Is very important for a capital intensive business.

Generally Accepted Standard:
Very broad range and must be viewed on a business's expectations. In general between 3 and 5 times.

Low Ratio:
The assets may not be fully employed or too many assets may be chasing too few sales.

High Ratio:
In general, the higher the ratio, the smaller the investment needed to generate sales which means greater profitability.

Remarks:
This ratio should only be used to compare firms within the same industry group and in conjunction with other ratios. As with any ratio measuring assets, it can give a distorted reading if the assets are heavily depreciated. Be careful when comparing two firms or comparing with industry averages that the asset figures are approximately the same.

XYZ HARDWARE AND BUILDING SUPPLY BALANCE SHEET
DECEMBER 31, YEAR

ASSETS			LIABILITIES	
Current Assets			Current Liabilities	
Cash	$ 2,000		Accounts Payable	$ 18,000
Accounts Receivable	85,000		Notes Payable	65,000
Inventory	210,000		Accruals	95,000
Total Current Assets	**$ 297,000**		**Total Current Liabilities**	**$ 178,000**
Fixed Assets			Long Term Liabilities	
Land	$ 50,000		Long Term Debt	$ 144,000
Equipment	50,000		**Total Liabilities**	**$ 322,000**
Furniture & Fixtures	25,000			
Total Fixed Assets	**$ 125,000**		Net Worth	$ 100,000
Total Assets	**$ 422,000**		**Total Liabilities**	
			and Net Worth	**$ 422,000**

XYZ HARDWARE AND BUILDING SUPPLY INCOME STATEMENT
FOR YEAR ENDING DECEMBER 31, YEAR

Net Sales (less allowances)		$ 700,000
Cost of Goods Sold		500,000
Gross (Margin) Profit		**$ 200,000**
Expenses		
Salaries	$ 130,000	
Freight	7,000	
Bad Debt	4,000	
Utilities	7,000	
Depreciation	4,000	
Insurance	7,000	
Taxes (local)	8,000	
Advertising	3,000	
Interest	10,000	
Miscellaneous	4,200	
Total Operating Expenses		**$ 184,200**
Operating Income		$ 15,800
Other Income		500
Income Before Taxes		**$ 16,300**

Fixed Asset Turnover Ratio

$$\frac{\text{Net Sales}}{\text{Fixed Assets}} = \frac{\$700,000}{\$125,000} = 5.6{:}1 \text{ or } 5.6 \text{ Times}$$

Summary of Efficiency Ratios

➤ Efficiency ratios measure how well you are conducting your business.

➤ Efficiency ratios help you keep your business in balance.

➤ Your accounts receivable times 365 days divided by your credit sales will tell you the length of time it takes your average customers to pay their bills.

➤ Dividing the cost of goods sold by your average inventory will provide you with the number of times you replace your inventory per month or year.

➤ Your net sales divided by your fixed assets will tell you how well you are generating sales in relation to your fixed assets.

Ratio 4: Market Ratios

Market ratios refer to financial calculations used by investors to evaluate the financial performance of publicly traded corporations. Three market ratios of particular interest to common stockholders are discussed below. Although these ratios are not particularly relevant to small businesses, a discussion of financial statements would not be complete without them.

These ratios measure whether the price of a share of common stock in a particular company is high or low when compared with that company's stock price trend as well as with other stocks available at the same time. Comparison of ratios for other companies within the same business sector can be very valuable to any ratio analysis.

Note: The following is an introduction to three market ratios. This initial discussion does not provide sufficient tools for investment decision-making. It is an introduction only and readers are advised to seek additional information prior to making investments in any company.

Market Ratios (CONTINUED)

Earnings Per Share

$$\frac{Net\ Earnings}{Average\ Shares\ Common\ Stock\ Outstanding}$$

Measures:
The net income for the period divided by the average number of common shares outstanding.

Low Ratio:
Either limited net earnings due to sluggish sales or high costs and/or a large number of common shares outstanding. Start-up companies or those with products still in development generally have low earnings per share, if any.

High Ratio:
Mature companies and/or those with limited shares of common stock outstanding.

Remarks:
Is very dependent on the economy in general, the specific industry, the age of the company and the number of common shares outstanding.

Common stockholders consider a decrease in earnings per share to be unfavorable. A decline in earnings per share generally indicates a decline in the profitability of the company and raises concerns about the company's future growth and profitability. Alternately, an increase in earnings per share is considered positive as long as the increase keeps up with market expectations.

Price/Earnings Ratio (P/E)

$$\frac{\textit{Market price of a share of common stock}}{\textit{Earnings per share of common stock}}$$

Measures:
The price of a share of common stock divided by the earnings per share of common stock. The P/E ratio represents the "multiple" that the market places on the earnings of a company.

Low Ratio:
Market perception that company will have minimal future earnings growth.

High Ratio:
Market perception of high future earnings or high growth potential.

Remarks:
The P/E ratio is the most commonly used ratio for evaluating a company today. The P/E ratio of most stocks has varied widely in recent years ranging from a low of about 10 to a high of over 50. The outlook for future earnings is the major factor influencing a company's P/E ratio.

The P/E ratio is used to compare companies within the same business sector or that are similar in nature. By using this ratio, investors can determine which company within an industry to invest in. For instance, the P/E ratios for two automobile manufacturers are 15 and 18 respectively. Assuming that the companies have similar future earnings potential, an investment in the company with the lower P/E ratio of 15 will generate greater future earnings potential for an investor.

The P/E ratios for many publicly traded companies are given in the business section of most daily newspapers. Remember that since the price of stocks can change daily, the P/E ratio will change daily as well.

Market Ratios (CONTINUED)

Dividend Yield

$$\frac{Dividends\ per\ share\ of\ common\ stock}{Market\ price\ per\ share\ of\ common\ stock}$$

Measures:
The relationship between cash dividends paid to common shareholders and the market price per share of common stock.

Low Ratio:
Low rate of return on stock investment. Perhaps could increase return by selling stock and purchasing higher yielding investment.

High Ratio:
Good investment. As long as dividend yield remains high, no need to change investment.

Remarks:
Dividends are of importance to shareholders who rely on corporate dividends for regular cash income. In general, the higher the dividend yield, the lower the capital gain through rising stock price.

Investors respond very negatively when a company reduces its dividends. Generally a reduced dividend payout is followed by a decline in the market price per share of stock.

This ratio is best used to compare companies with relatively stable stock prices for two reasons. First, a company with a wildly fluctuating stock price does not provide as meaningful a yield ratio. Second, these types of stocks are intended for long-term returns, not the increase in capital gain.

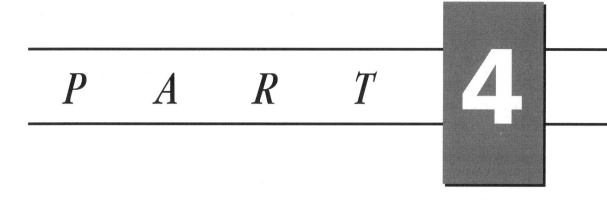

PART 4

How to Perform a
Ratio Analysis

Introduction

Now that you have learned what ratios are and what they can do for you, we are ready to learn how to organize and use ratios analyzing a business. This section will provide forms and charts that will help you collect, organize and evaluate a business through the use of a ratio review chart.

Data Collection Charts

The Data Gathering Form and the Comparison Chart, will help you organize your ratios (blank forms are provided on pages 62 and 63) and assist you in using the Ratio Review Chart on page 65.

The Data Gathering Form provides a means of collecting the necessary figures from the balance sheet and the profit and loss statement.

The Comparison Chart provides space to work your ratios and insert your industry averages. Industry average figures are compiled by several sources. Some names and addresses of where to find industry average data are listed in the Appendix. This information may be purchased, but it is usually available through a banker, library, small business association office, Chamber of Commerce or the Internet. Your trade association may also compile similar statistics both nationally and regionally. Regional numbers may be more appropriate for your use.

To make the best of these forms, make several copies and use them by filling in the blanks from your balance sheet and profit and loss statement. Examples of filled in forms are shown on the following pages. These samples are based on the same balance sheet and profit and loss statement we have been using.

What Is Significant?

To determine which ratios to use, consider the type of business you have, the age of your business, the point in the business cycle and what you are looking for. For instance, one type of business might require a large number of fixed assets, buildings, land, equipment, tools, etc. while another requires very few. The significant ratios in the first case would be those that help you measure how well you are using your fixed assets.

Another type of business may need to carry a well-stocked inventory or perhaps just enough to satisfy emergency needs. In either case, inventory turnover is critical, and if it gets out of hand, you may not be able to pay current expenses on the one hand, or have the stock to satisfy your customers on the other.

The age of your business is important. If you have passed the initial three to five year start-up period and have liquidity, you are probably interested in expansion. In this case, the profitability and efficiency ratios will be factors you need to closely monitor. Be careful to keep your business operations in balance.

Some businesses are dependent upon seasonality for their income. That is, more sales occur during certain periods of the year than any other. During each rise and fall of this cycle, ratios can be quite different. It becomes necessary to watch these periods so your ratios reflect what is needed. For example, if you are expecting a big sale, but it hasn't come through, or anticipating a low sales period, you will need liquidity to carry you through. If you sell on credit, you will need to watch your collection time between the sale and the payment, or you will face a lack of working capital.

Finally, if you are planning for expansion, you should be able to show regular profits which are in line with your industry. A low debt structure will also help influence lenders to provide the money you need at a favorable interest rate.

DATA GATHERING FORM

Business name: XYZ Hardware and Building Supply
Business address: Anywhere U.S.A.
Date prepared: month/day/year

Items	Dollar Figures
Current Assets	$297,000
Current Liabilities	$178,000
Net Sales	$700,000
Working Capital	$119,000
Total Debt	$322,000
Net Worth/Equity	$100,000
Operating Income	$15,800
Income Before Taxes	$16,300
Total Assets	$422,000
Accounts Receivable	$85,000
Cost of Goods Sold	$500,000
Average Inventory	$210,000
Fixed Assets	$125,000

COMPARISON CHART

Business name: XYZ Hardware and Building Supply
Business address: Anywhere U.S.A.
Date prepared: month/day/year

Ratio Title	Ratios	Dollar Figures	My Ratios	Industry Average**
Current Ratio	Current Assets / Current Liabilities	$297,000 / $178,000	1.7 times	1.8 times
Turnover of Cash	Net Sales / Working Capital	$700,000 / $119,000	5.9 times	11.9 times
Debt to Equity	Total Debt / Net Worth	$322,000 / $100,000	3.2 times	1.9 times
Rate of Return on Sales	Operating Income / Net Sales	$15,800 / $700,000	2.3%	Not Available
ROA	Income Before Taxes / Total Assets	$16,300 / $422,000	3.9%	5.7%
ROI	Income Before Taxes / Net Worth	$16,300 / $100,000	16.3%	31.5%
Average Collection Period	Acct's Rec'ble x 365 / Net Sales	$85,000 x 365 / $700,000	44 days	33 days
Inventory Turnover	Cost of Goods Sold / Average Inventory	$500,000 / $210,000	2.4 times	7.2 times
Fixed Asset Turnover	Net Sales / Fixed Assets	$700,000 / $125,000	5.6 times	29.2 times

* Not all ratios are listed by all sources. The absence of one or two ratios should not significantly affect your analysis.

** See Appendix.

DATA GATHERING FORM

Business name: _____

Business address: _____

Date prepared: _____

Items	Dollar Figures
Current Assets	
Current Liabilities	
Net Sales	
Working Capital	
Total Debt	
Net Worth/Equity	
Operating Income	
Income Before Taxes	
Total Assets	
Accounts Receivable	
Cost of Goods Sold	
Average Inventory	
Fixed Assets	

(Note: This form may be copied by permission of the publisher)

COMPARISON CHART

Business name: _____

Business address: _____

Date prepared: _____

Ratio Title	Ratios	Dollar Figures	My Ratios	Industry Average
Current Ratio	Current Assets / Current Liabilities			
Turnover of Cash	Net Sales / Working Capital			
Debt to Equity	Total Debt / Net Worth			
Rate of Return of Sales	Operating Income / Net Sales			
ROA	Income Before Taxes / Total Assets			
ROI	Income Before Taxes / Net Worth			
Average Collection Period	Acct's Rec'ble x 365 / Net Sales			
Inventory Turnover	Cost of Goods Sold / Average Inventory			
Fixed Asset Turnover	Net Sales / Fixed Assets			

(Note: This form may be copied by permission of the publisher)

Ratio Review Chart

The chart on the next two pages provides a quick look at how your business is doing. You may discover things to check into because a ratio is too low. The page number for each ratio is listed to help refresh your memory of what each ratio means and how it is derived.

This review chart is more to help stimulate your thinking and not necessarily to provide answers. To make the best use of it make several copies and complete one each month with those ratios you feel are most important for your business. Please note that your industry averages are normally published quarterly so you may not have them for a month-to-month comparison. However, this chart can provide quick comparisons, and progress can be charted to help keep your business in balance.

Remember, things take time; don't try for too big a correction too quickly as such a move may cause problems in other areas.

RATIO REVIEW CHART

Ratio	Your Ratio	Ind Avg*	If Your Ratio is High	If Your Ratio is Low
Current Assets / Current Liabilities (Pages 30-31)			Check your debt, savings accts., inventory, etc., to see that your money is working for you.	Check inventory, accts rec, and debt structure to see if you can obtain more cash.
Net Sales / Working Capital (Pages 32-33)			Check the ratio above; see if you can obtain more cash.	You may have a cash surplus; invest it in the business, in savings or pay debts.
Total Debt / Net Worth (Pages 34-35)			Check your debt structure.	If too low, you should consider borrowing if the payback is right.
Operating Income / Net Sales (Pages 38-39)			Generally, keep up the good work.	Check expenses and sales expectations.
Income Before Taxes / Total Assets (Pages 40-41)			Generally, keep up the good work.	Check your operating policy for asset use.
Income Before Taxes / Net Worth (Pages 42-43)			Check your net worth structure, you could be undercapitalized or a good manager.	Check your debt structure, expenses or operating policies.

RATIO REVIEW CHART (CONTINUED)

Ratio	Your Ratio	Ind Avg*	If Your Ratio is High	If Your Ratio is Low
Acct's Rec'ble x 365 / Net Sales (Pages 46-47)			Check your credit policy.	Generally, keep up the good work.
Cost of Goods Sold / Average Inventory (Pages 48-49)			Could be a good sign; check inventory and unfilled sales orders.	Check for overstocking or obsolete items; check cash flow.
Net Sales / Fixed Assets (Pages 50-51)			Generally, keep up the good work.	Check necessity for all assets; check if sales can't be increased.

* IND AVG = Industry Average

Note: _____

These ratio charts do not take into account the age of a business, the time of the business cycle, local or national economic conditions, or any specific mixes of business. You should consider any one or more of these conditions at the time you are analyzing your business.

(Note: This form may be copied by permission of the publisher.)

Afterword

If One Ratio Goes Up Will Another Always Go Down?

Sometimes they do. But ratios generally don't work out so neatly.

Sometimes two or more ratios indicate good work and both will be high. Sometimes, depending on your type of business or the time in your business cycle, one will be low, or it won't make any difference what a ratio does.

Ratios are tools to help you analyze a business. In the next two parts of this book you will be introduced to other techniques that will help you keep your business in balance. It is important to remember that all tools will never be used all the time. If ratios are used improperly, it could worsen your position.

The proper use of ratios also takes into consideration the economy, the business cycle and whether your business is just getting started, is achieving growth or has reached maturity.

Think It Through!

Summary of Part 4

➤ The first step in determining the interaction between ratios is to record the proper dollar figures for the appropriate item (i.e. sales, net profit) from your balance sheet and profit and loss statement to the data gathering form.

➤ The second step is to transfer the dollar figures from the data gathering form to the comparison chart then determine your ratios and place them on the chart.

➤ The third step is to look up your industry ratio averages and place them on the comparison chart.

➤ The fourth step is to transfer your ratios and the industry averages to the ratio review chart and compare how your ratios match up with those of your industry. The ratio review chart will provide you a quick, cursory means of determining what corrective action you should take.

➤ The fifth step is to plan how to get those of yours that are off back on track .... and do it!

➤ All ratios will not be significant to you all the time.

➤ Ratios will react differently depending on your business' age, the time in the business cycle, the economic conditions and your type of business.

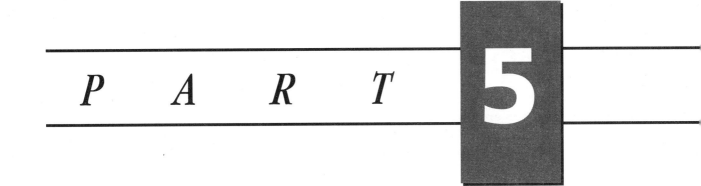

PART 5

How to Perform an Expense Analysis

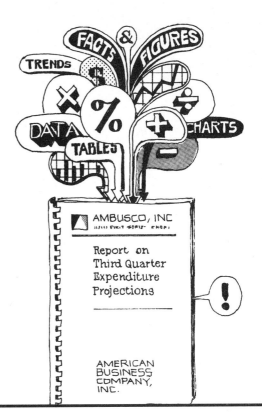

Is Anything Good About Expenses?

Expenses are a necessary part of doing business and should be treated as such. Expenses should not to be feared or denied. Expenses, however, must be taken into account when developing pricing policies, sales expectations, and a business plan.

Expenses are a fact of life for any business. But expenses that are too high will quickly ruin a business. This may seem obvious, but the point is: expenses must be controlled. The best way to do this is by understanding them; knowing what will result when you increase or decrease an expense.

Examining Your Expenses

Being familiar with and regularly examining your expenses, will help you every day that you are in business. Good expense control can help you maximize profits on the same or even fewer sales.

A good examination begins with the sales line on your profit and loss statement, P & L. Understanding why sales did or did not occur as projected will put you in a better position to understand how the expenses of doing business behaved as they did. The first thing to note is whether a particular event happened that month, such as an unusually large sale. Perhaps what should have been a slow month suddenly became a strong one. Or vice-versa, perhaps bad weather caused shipments to be late and sales suffered. If you were unaware of factors affecting sales, you might overbuy inventory after an abnormal non-recurring sale. This could cause you to lose profits later on if you have to cut prices to move an aging inventory.

The Sales Line

Sales dollars or income is a function of unit price times unit volume. Therefore, an increase in either will increase sales dollars. Likewise, if either decreases (with no offsetting increase in the other parameter), sales dollars will drop. Marking down the price without an offsetting increase in volume will result in lower revenue and almost always a loss of profit. If you planned to take a trade discount to increase your inventory for a special sale and money wasn't available in time to take your discount, then when the merchandise arrived and the customers didn't, there would be double trouble.

The Cost Of Goods Sold

The next item to evaluate while examining expenses is the cost of goods sold. Be sensitive to any increase or decrease as a percentage of net sales. Find causes for either an increase or decrease such as: purchased items that increased or decreased in price. Perhaps it is something like increased freight charges, spoilage, or shrinkage due to theft. This area often seems like a "so what" sort of category, but the success of many businesses can be determined by paying attention and sweating the details on the cost of goods sold line.

The cost of goods sold should be broken down into specific line items such as: freight in, manufacturing costs, discounts (taken or not taken), etc. A good review should include going through current invoices and comparing them with past invoices for the same merchandise to determine where the variances are and what caused them.

Examining Your Expenses (CONTINUED)

Credits And Collections

There is a cost in making money. The trick is to shorten the time between commitment of cash and the collection of cash. One of the best ways is to continually review expenses.

Fixed Expenses (Expenses whether or not a sale is made)

Let's move on to fixed expenses such as rent, interest, insurance, depreciation, taxes, and licenses. Each fixed expense should be spread in equal monthly installments for the year. If this is done, an increase in sales should cause profit margins to increase at a faster rate than if costs were variable (i.e., tied to sales). Fixed expenses can produce a greater return from increased sales than variable expenses. The reverse is also true if sales decrease and expenses are fixed and can't be reduced. Control of expenses, especially fixed expenses, should include the following:

1. Negotiate the best price for all products and services you purchase at the beginning. Use competitive bidding!

2. Try bartering.

3. Pay only as much and as often as you have to, continually look for better prices.

4. Never pay early.

5. Assume that all payment terms are negotiable.

6. Invest—don't spend.

Variable Expenses (Tied to sales volume)

Variable expenses may include salaries, advertising costs, delivery, supplies, telephone, dues and subscriptions, and utilities. These costs should be analyzed in relation to their return on sales or other cost efficiencies. They are comparable with the "year-to-date" figures and percentages. These percentages should be in line with industry percentages and past experience. If sales rise or fall and action is not taken to adjust expenses, closer examination is necessary.

By carefully analyzing variable expenses you can determine their value in relation to creating sales or increasing margin. This is vital when forecasting, planning new product lines, or expansion, etc..

At the bottom of the statement is net profit. Net profit may look okay, but there still may be trouble because of other variables. If some expense items were reduced and the profit margin did not rise, then something else occurred to offset the logical profit increase. There may be trouble in the cost of goods sold, for example. Remember that it's *collected dollars*, not sales dollars, that you take to the bank. **Don't confuse profits with cash flow**.

Increase the Return on Expenses

When you run out of cost-cutting ideas, try increasing the return on your expenses. This can be done in several ways including:

1. Examining your credit policy. Do you:

- ❏ Invoice promptly?
- ❏ Provide clear information about your terms and collection policies?
- ❏ Maintain a receivables aging schedule and conduct a prompt follow-up on delinquent customers?
- ❏ Carefully check credit references?

2. Examining your cash pay-outs. Do you:

- ❏ Take advantage of trade discounts?
- ❏ Pay bills only when they are due?
- ❏ Try to establish extended terms with creditors to your advantage, such as expended dating or paying your debt over a long period of time?
- ❏ Buy only what is needed—when it is needed?
- ❏ Check petty cash flow?

3. Examining your payroll. Do you:

- ❏ Before hiring a new employee consider: overtime? part-time help? temporary help? or free-lance workers?
- ❏ Pay all of your employees on the same day?
- ❏ Consider reducing your salary during slack periods and increasing it during better times?
- ❏ Check the amount of "downtime" caused by equipment or other controllable items?
- ❏ Check starting and quitting times?
- ❏ Check length of break times and personal times?

4. Examining your inventory controls. Do you:

- ❏ Check your security to prevent theft?

- ❏ Instruct your employees about proper handling and storage to prevent breakage and damage to inventory?

- ❏ Calculate in the cost of inventory, the cost of storage, handling, insurance, taxes, deterioration, obsolescence, etc. to ensure you aren't fooling yourself?

- ❏ Do you regularly check the turnover rate to see if your inventory can't be reduced?

- ❏ Look into just-in-time inventory (i.e. keep your inventory levels to a logical minimum)?

- ❏ Always calculate a level of inventory relative to your needs?

5. Examining your manufacturing. Do you:

- ❏ Get competitive bids from contractors?

- ❏ Look into contracting with smaller, less expensive "Cottage Suppliers"?

- ❏ Tighten up planning and scheduling?

- ❏ Keep high quality standards? (Rework can be more costly.)

6. Examining your marketing plan. Do you:

- ❏ Avoid a "shotgun" approach to advertising and instead target your specific customer group?

- ❏ Have a clear policy on returns and repairs?

- ❏ Make sure discounts are going to work, and have a way to end them if they don't?

- ❏ Train salespeople to sell accessory items?

- ❏ Demand quality, courteous service for your customers?

- ❏ Train employees dealing directly with customers to maximize their positive initial impact?

Increase the Return on Expenses (CONTINUED)

7. Examining your purchasing costs. Do you:

- ❑ Control the items purchased to necessities?

- ❑ Ensure all major purchases are competitively bid?

- ❑ Eliminate unprofitable products from your line?

- ❑ Look for more efficient ways to "build" your product?

- ❑ Maintain good working relationships with your vendors?

8. Other areas to examine. Do you:

- ❑ Use customer furnished material? Barter?

- ❑ Avoid early payment of expenses (e.g. a year's supply of _____ or a three-year payment of insurance, etc.?)

- ❑ Avoid unnecessary improvements?

- ❑ Avoid unnecessary volume purchases?

- ❑ Keep good records?

- ❑ Make cash deposits daily, investing surplus funds in interest bearing accounts?

Summary of Part 5

➤ Expenses are a normal part of doing business and should be considered as such.

➤ Expenses can and should be controlled so you will know what you are getting for them.

➤ Begin your expense examination by analyzing sales.

➤ Next look at cost of goods sold. See if it has increased or decreased, and then find out why.

➤ Fixed expenses should not vary significantly with any increase or decrease in sales.

➤ Variable expenses may change with your sales volume.

➤ When you think you have cut expenses to the bone, there are eight major areas of your business you can examine to increase your return on expenses (pages 74-76).

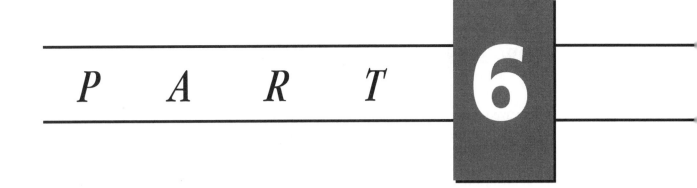

How to Control

Your Business

How To Proceed

There are several ways to control your business. Some of the best ones involve financial analysis. The following pages will bring together the use of ratios and percentages and present four basic techniques to help you control your business.

By control, we are talking not only about meeting industry averages, but about helping you forecast how much money it will take to prepare for a big promotional sale, or introduce a new product line or expand your sales. Control works two ways. First, it helps you improve what you are now doing and second, it helps you prepare for expansion or change without being caught short of cash because you did not have a plan to keep things in balance.

The four techniques to be introduced are:

1. **Trend analysis**

2. **Cash position charting**

3. **Target statements**

4. **Accounts receivable aging schedule**

We will consider each individually.

Trend Analysis

The Data Gathering Form and the Comparison Chart which were introduced earlier will aid you in doing a trend analysis. A trend analysis is simply a method of keeping track of month-to-month and year to year ratios and expenses. It helps you stay on the right path by alerting you to adjustments you need to make to operate your business successfully.

Four charts found at the end of this section will help you do this. The first keeps track of your ratios month-to-month. The second is for tracking your year-to-year ratios. The third is for month-to-month expense tracking. And the fourth is for tracking your year-to-year expenses.

Make a copy of each monthly chart at the beginning of your business year. Label each column with the appropriate name of the month. Record the month ending ratios or expenses in the proper column and you will soon have a monthly trend that you can study. Recording year-end ratios and expenses on a yearly chart will build a yearly trend for you. The last column on the chart should list your goals or industry averages for each ratio or expense percent. This will allow you to chart how well you are progressing toward your goals.

By keeping track, you have a history of how well you are doing. These records are great for review and analysis and will help you plan future action.

The next two charts (pages 82 and 86) are examples of how you can use trends to better understand your business. In our first example, the ratio comparison chart provides a three-year look at the XYZ Hardware and Building Supply Company. Our assumption is that the owner is trying to match or come close to the column labeled IND AVG (which stands for industry averages).

XYZ HARDWARE AND BUILDING SUPPLY
RATIO COMPARISON
THREE YEARS

Ratio	1st year	2nd year	3rd year	Ind Ave
Current Assets / Current Liabilities	1.7 x	1.9 x	1.9 x	1.8 x
Net Sales / Working Capital	5.9 x	6.5 x	6.7 x	11.9 x
Total Debt / Net Worth	3.2 x	2.5 x	2.0 x	1.9 x
Operating Income / Net Sales	2.3%	3%	2.3%	Not available
Income Before Taxes / Total Assets	3.9%	.8%	4.4%	5.7%
Income Before Taxes / Net Worth	16.3%	3.2%	18.4%	31.5%
Acct's Rec'ble x 365 / Net Sales	4 days	38 days	46 days	33 days
Cost of Goods Sold / Average Inventory	2.4 x	3.7 x	4.0 x	7.2 x
Net Sales / Fixed Assets	5.6 x	8.0 x	10.0 x	29.2 x

Note: x = Times; % = Percent;

Days = average number of days it takes to collect credit sales;

Ind Avg = industry average. The industry average ratios shown are the median ratios taken from the 1998 Annual Statement Studies, asset size 0-500M,

Retailers—Builders Materials, SIC# 5211, copyright by Robert Morris Associates, used with permission.

  * Not all ratios are listed by all sources. The absence of one or two ratios should not significantly affect your analysis.

 ** Please note the disclaimer and other information in the Appendix.

AUTHOR COMMENTS

XYZ Hardware and Building Supply Ratio Comparison Analysis

It appears that the current asset to liabilities ratio is moving in the right direction as is sales to working capital. Total debt to net worth is above the industry average but is closing in on a recommended figure. The earnings fell sharply in year two, primarily due to increased salaries. The third year shows improvement as salaries fall nearer to industry norms. The return on investment, however, rose, then fell, and remains short of the average.

If the owner wished to get earnings before taxes up to the 31.5% average, he or she could increase sales and/or decrease expenses. Continuing on, the income before taxes to total assets is also rising in year three, and is approaching the average. Collection of credit sales were moving in the right direction, then slipped. Perhaps the owner extended the credit terms to increase sales. The inventory turnover is moving in the right direction but remains below the industry average, which probably means that the company is still overstocked. The cash position hasn't changed much.

The turnover of sales to fixed assets is moving toward the average, but still lags behind. This may be due to high inventory or more sales need to be generated for the amount of assets employed. This ratio should be run using total assets to see if they are in line.

So there is both good news and bad news for the XYZ Company but overall, progress is being made. As you review your trends you will want to check back to your original balance sheets and profit and loss statements, so be sure to save them. The next page summarizes the XYZ analysis and suggests actions to improve the business results.

Author Recommendations

Recommended actions to be taken by the XYZ Hardware and Building Supply Company include:

1. Reducing debt by replacing the inventory only when absolutely necessary. Apply the savings to pay off notes or the mortgage faster. The money gained from speeding up the collection of receivables can also be used to reduce debt. The reduction of debt should increase net worth because debt should decrease faster than current assets. The reduction of inventory and accounts receivable should help the net profit to total asset ratio.

2. Speeding up the collection of receivables will lower the average days' collection period. If credit terms were previously extended to increase sales, it doesn't appear to have helped. If this was done, credit terms need to be changed (i.e., tightened).

3. Slowing down stock purchasing. The inventory turnover ratio should improve.

4. Shrinking fixed assets should improve the sales to fixed assets ratio. However, increasing sales is a better way to do it.

Now let's see how expenses are measuring up.

AUTHOR COMMENTS

XYZ Hardware and Building Supply Expense Analysis

The cost of goods sold ratio is holding steady and is lower than the industry average, even as sales climb. Sales have increased each year by over 3%, but gross profit did not keep pace. This could be attributed to the owner not taking advantage of volume discounts or trade discounts or perhaps this is the nature of the business. The company could also be losing sales since their gross margin is higher than the industry average. Salary expense increased dramatically in year two but dropped back in year three. This could account for the lack of working capital the second year and why the profitability ratios were so low in year two. Employee salaries are coming in line with the industry average the third year. Salary expense should be watched to ensure the trend does not reverse itself.

Bad debt expense is close to average. The drop in bad debt the third year may indicate better credit control and should be encouraged. Utility, depreciation, and insurance payments seem high compared to the industry average and should be checked to see if the amount of coverage is really necessary. Meeting the industry average for insurance alone would add over $1,000 to profit. Taxes are also high and cost the company over $8,000 per year. Advertising is low but sales are rising. Sales may go up faster with more publicity. Net profit is falling in spite of rising sales, but is above the industry average.

AUTHOR RECOMMENDATIONS

1. Check gross profit by investigating volume and/or trade discounts.

2. Keep up the good work on holding expenses.

3. Check into insurance payments and taxes to see if these items could be lowered.

4. And keep a eye on employee expenses as sales rise.

XYZ HARDWARE AND BUILDING SUPPLY RATIO COMPARISON THREE YEARS							
Expense Item	**1st year**		**2nd year**		**3rd year**		**Ind Ave**
	$$ AM'T	%	$$ AM'T	%	$$ AM'T	%	%
Sales	700,000	100	725,000	100	750,000	100	100
CGS	500,000	71.4	522,000	72	540,000	72	75
Gross Profit	200,000	28.6	203,000	28	210,000	28	25
% Inc. in Sales		3.6		3.4			
Salaries*	130,000	18.6	143,000	19.7	139,000	18.4	14.7
Freight	7,000	1.0	11,000	1.5	9,000	1.2	N/A
Bad Debt	4,000	.6	4,000	.6	3,000	.5	.3
Utilities	7,000	1.0	7,000	.9	7,600	1.0	.4
Depreciation	4,000	.6	4,000	.6	4,000	.5	1.0
Insurance	7,000	1.0	7,000	.9	7,500	1.0	.6
Taxes (local)	8,000	1.1	8,500	1.2	8,000	1.1	.2
Advertising	3,000	.4	3,500	.5	3,700	.5	.7
Interest	10,000	1.4	8,000	1.1	5,200	1.1	1.0
Miscellaneous**	4,200	.6	4,500	.6	5,500	.7	4.0
	184,200	26.3	200,500	27.7	192,500	25.7	23.0
Oper. Income	15,800	2.3	2,500	.3	17,500	2.3	1.8
Other Income	500	0	700	.1	900	.1	.6
Inc. Before Tax	16,300	2.3	3,200	.4	18,400	2.5	2.4

Note: $$ AM'T = Dollar Amount; Ind Avg = industry average; CGS = cost of goods sold; % Inc in Sales = percent increase in sales each year; N/A = not available; Oper. Income = operating income; Other Income = interest; Inc. Before Tax = income before taxes. Expense industry averages are from the 1998 Cost of Doing Business Study, copyright by the National Retail Hardware Association, Indianapolis, IN. Used with permission.

 * Salaries includes owners,officers, and all other employees, salaries, bonuses, payroll taxes and benefits.

** Miscellaneous includes office and shop supplies, building repair and maintenance, rent or ownership in real estate, leasing, legal and accounting, computer services, dues and subscriptions, entertainment, laundry, disposal and other.

AUTHOR COMMENTS

A yearly example was used for this analysis, but it could have been monthly. In your analysis you should do both, since most businesses rise and fall substantially during a year's business cycle and comparing similar months year-by-year can be useful.

End-of-year figures are most commonly used to make trend charts. But if one particular month in your business cycle provides a more meaningful point in time, use that month as your starting point for yearly figures. Remember to start with the same month each time you prepare your yearly chart to make comparisons meaningful.

These numbers must be coupled with honest experience and common sense to be of value. A ratio consists of two figures. To change it you can raise one, lower the other, or do both. There is usually more than one choice. Before taking action, check (using target numbers) to see what effect your action may have on other ratios as some figures are used in more than one ratio. Following this page, there are the four blank forms (pages 88-91), which you may copy and use to analyze your trends.

Note: Forms on pages 88-91 may be copied by permission of the publisher

RATIO COMPARISON BY MONTH

Business name: _____

Business address: _____

Ratio	Month						
Current Assets / Current Liabilities							
Net Sales / Working Capital							
Total Debt / Net Worth							
Operating Income / Net Sales							
Income Before Taxes / Total Assets							
Income Before Taxes / Net Worth							
Accts Rec'ble x 365 / Net Sales							
Cost of Goods Sold / Average Inventory							
Net Sales / Fixed Assets							

Ratio Comparison By Year

Business name: _____

Business address: _____

Ratio	Year						
Current Assets / Current Liabilities							
Net Sales / Working Capital							
Total Debt / Net Worth							
Operating Income / Net Sales							
Income Before Taxes / Total Assets							
Income Before Taxes / Net Worth							
Accts Rec'ble x 365 / Net Sales							
Cost of Goods Sold / Average Inventory							
Net Sales / Fixed Assets							

EXPENSE COMPARISON BY MONTH

Business name: _____

Business address: _____

Month							
Expense Item	$$ AM'T	%	$$ AM'T	%	$$ AM'T	%	Ind Avg
Sales							
CGS							
Gross Profit							
% Inc (Dec) in Sales							
Drawings (Owner)							
Wages							
Delivery							
Bad Debt							
Telephone							
Depreciation							
Insurance							
Taxes (local)							
Interest							
Advertising							
Miscellaneous							
Net Profit Before Taxes							

Expense Comparison By Year

Business name: _____

Business address: _____

Year							
Expense Item	$$ AM'T	%	$$ AM'T	%	$$ AM'T	%	Ind Avg
Sales							
CGS							
Gross Profit							
% Inc (Dec) in Sales							
Drawings (Owner)							
Wages							
Delivery							
Bad Debt							
Telephone							
Depreciation							
Insurance							
Taxes (local)							
Interest							
Advertising							
Miscellaneous							
Net Profit Before Taxes							

Cash Position Charting

If there is only one thing you remember from this book, make it this: **Never run out of cash!**

In a small business operation a lack of cash, even for a short time, can cause all of your work and planning to become worthless. A cash shortage is the one thing that is most difficult to overcome. If you can't pay your bills, your help, or yourself, you won't be in business very long *even if you are showing a paper profit!*

To help avoid this situation especially when planning to do something different, a cash position chart will be of immeasurable value. This chart will help you target when cash will be needed to pay bills. It will also help you determine where to obtain cash to support items like expansion (such as speeding up receivables collection, increasing cash sales, or borrowing). The cash position chart deals only with cash—cash paid out and cash taken in. It helps identify those periods when borrowing must be considered. This allows you to make arrangements for the cash before you actually need it. Pre-planning is especially helpful when talking with bankers.

An estimated cash position chart should be made a year in advance. A second chart should be used to record actual cash income and outgo on a weekly or monthly basis. By keeping track of outflow and inflow of cash and comparing these actual figures to your estimates, your budgeting ability will greatly improve. You will have good documents to show if you need to seek new money. Another version would be to make two columns for each month, one would be for the estimate the other would be for the actual. This method has the advantage of checking the accuracy of your estimates on one chart. Both types of charts are shown at the end of this section. The cash position chart on page 94 shows estimates for the beginning month plus the next five months.

In making your cash position chart, follow the example on page 94. In the first column, list starting cash that you believe will be available at the end of the beginning month. In the example shown, it is $200. Next, list the cash sales at the end of the month ($3,550 in our example). Then list the cash received from previous sales ($550 in our example) in the beginning month. This provides a total cash-in of $4,100.

To determine cash-out, list what you believe your expenses will be. In the example the expenses are: $1,000 purchases, $600 rent, $2,050 wages and $350 for miscellaneous expenses, for a total cash-out of $4,000. Next add total cash-in to the starting cash balance and then subtract the total cash-out to obtain the ending balance, which is $300 in the example.

The cash position is found by subtracting the total cash-out from the total cash-in, or $100. Here we are interested only in the amount of cash generated or lost during the beginning month. A loss is shown with the dollar figure between ( ), i.e. as a loss of $25 would be shown as (25).

Take the ending balance and place it at the top of the chart as the first month's starting cash figure. In our example this is $300. Then record the end of the month totals for cash-in and cash-out. The ending balance comes from adding the starting cash, $300, to the cash-in, $3,450, for a balance of $3,750, and subtracting total cash-out from it (3,950) for an ending balance in the first month of a negative $200, shown as (200). The cash flow for the first month is cash-out subtracted from cash-in, or a negative $500, shown as (500).

The first month's ending balance becomes the second month's starting cash (a negative $200). After the second month's ending totals are written in, our example shows that the ending balance is a positive $100. In other words, cash position has changed to a positive $300 and stays positive, as the cash sales and credit collections increase and expenses remain stable.

In the second month, the projected ending balance and cash position both become positive.

CASH POSITION CHART

ITEMS	MONTHS					
	Begin	**1st**	**2nd**	**3rd**	**4th**	**5th**
Starting Cash	200	300	(200)	100	400	600
Cash-in						
Cash Sales	3,550	2,950	4,000	3,300	3,000	3,200
Cash Received	550	500	1,550	1,800	2,000	2,000
Total Cash-in	4,100	3,450	5,550	5,100	5,000	5,200
Cash-out						
Purchases	1,000	1,000	2,500	2,000	2,000	2,000
Rent	600	600	600	600	600	600
Wages	2,050	2,050	2,050	2,050	2,050	2,050
Miscellaneous	350	300	100	150	150	150
Total Cash-out	4,000	3,950	5,250	4,800	4,800	4,800
Ending Balance	300	(200)	100	400	600	1,000
Cash Position	100	(500)	300	300	200	400

Note: ( ) means a loss or negative cash position. Your chart will be much more detailed than this example, which was shortened to simplify the explanation.

The cash position chart can also be used for planning cash positions, the following two examples (pages 95 and 96) provide a brief demonstration. For instance, you might want to consider borrowing instead of running a negative ending balance in the second month. The example on the facing page shows what would happen if you borrowed $200 in the beginning month.

Planning Cash Positions

Let's look at the example below. By starting with cash of $400, and keeping everything else the same, we see that there is no negative ending balance. But note the cash position is the same as in the example on page 94. This is because the difference between our cash-in and cash-out did not change. We start recording a positive cash position at the end of the second month as before.

CASH POSITION CHART

ITEMS	MONTHS					
	Begin	**1st**	**2nd**	**3rd**	**4th**	**5th**
Starting Cash	400	500	0	300	600	800
Cash-in						
Cash Sales	3,550	2,950	4,000	3,300	3,000	3,200
Cash Received	550	500	1,550	1,800	2,000	2,000
Total Cash-in	4,100	3,450	5,550	5,100	5,000	5,200
Cash-out						
Purchases	1,000	1,000	2,500	2,000	2,000	2,000
Rent	600	600	600	600	600	600
Wages	2,050	2,050	2,050	2,050	2,050	2,050
Miscellaneous	350	300	100	150	150	150
Total Cash-out	4,000	3,950	5,250	4,800	4,800	4,800
Ending Balance	500	0	300	600	800	1,200
Change in						
Cash Position	100	(500)	300	300	200	400

Note: * Assumes $200 has been borrowed

( ) means a loss or negative cash position.

Your chart will be much more detailed than this example which was shortened to simplify the explanation.

Interest paid on the loan would be an expense each month until paid. In this example it was not shown.

Cash Position Charting (CONTINUED)

If you didn't want to borrow but wanted a positive ending balance and cash position, you could collect your receivables faster, reduce expenses, or postpone other expenses such as hiring. To see what happens if we reduce purchasing by $500 in the first month and second month, study the example below. The ending balance stays positive. Cash flow breaks even in the first month and also stays positive. If purchases could be reduced (perhaps increased at a later date) there would not be a negative cash position and this action could keep your cash flow positive and your business healthy.

CASH POSITION CHART

ITEMS	MONTHS					
	Begin	**1st**	**2nd**	**3rd**	**4th**	**5th**
Starting Cash	200	300	300	1,100	1,400	1,600
Cash-In						
Cash Sales	3,550	2,950	4,000	3,300	3,000	3,200
Cash Received	550	500	1,550	1,800	2,000	2,000
Total Cash-In	**4,100**	**3,450**	**5,550**	**5,100**	**5,000**	**5,200**
Cash-Out						
Purchases	1,000	500	2,000	2,000	2,000	2,000
Rent	600	600	600	600	600	600
Wages	2,050	2,050	2,050	2,050	2,050	2,050
Miscellaneous	350	300	100	150	150	150
Total Cash-Out	**4,000**	**3,450**	**4,750**	**4,800**	**4,800**	**4,800**
Ending Balance	**300**	**300**	**1,100**	**1,400**	**1,600**	**2,000**
Cash Position	**100**	**0**	**800**	**300**	**200**	**400**

Note: ( ) means a loss or negative cash position.

Your chart will be much more detailed than this example, which was shortened to simplify the explanation.

By using a cash position chart you can keep your business solvent and learn your lessons on paper (not the hard way).

Pages 97 and 99 contain cash position charts. Improve your cash position by using one of them. These may be copied by permission of the publisher.

CASH POSITION CHART

Business name: _____

Business address: _____

Month:						
Beginning of Month Cash On Hand						
Cash in Bank						
Other Cash						
Total Cash						
Income During Month Cash Sales						
Credit Sales Receipts						
Investment Income						
Other Income						
Total Income						
Expenses During Month Purchases (Inventory)						
Owner's Drawings						
Salaries						
Taxes (Payroll)						
Repair/Maintenance						
Selling Expense						
Transportation						
Loan Payment						
Office Supplies						
Utilities						

Cash Position Chart (CONTINUED)

Month:						
Telephone						
Dues/Subscriptions						
Depreciation						
Advertising						
Rent						
Taxes						
Insurance						
Legal/Accounting						
Other						
Total Expenses End of Month						
End of Month Balance (Loss)						
Change in Cash Position Monthly						

CASH POSITION CHART

Business name: _____

Business address: _____

Month:	Budget	Actual	Budget	Actual	Budget	Actual
Beginning of Month Cash On Hand						
Cash in Bank						
Other Cash						
Total Cash						
Income During Month Cash Sales						
Credit Sales Receipts						
Investment Income						
Other Income						
Total Income						
Expenses During Month Purchases (Inventory)						
Owner's Drawings						
Salaries						
Taxes (Payroll)						
Repair/Maintenance						
Selling Expense						
Transportation						
Loan Payment						
Office Supplies						

Cash Position Chart (CONTINUED)

Month:	Budget	Actual	Budget	Actual	Budget	Actual
Utilities						
Telephone						
Dues/Subscriptions						
Depreciation						
Advertising						
Rent						
Taxes						
Insurance						
Legal/Accounting						
Other						
Total Expenses End of Month						
End of Month Balance (Loss)						
Change in Cash Position Monthly						

Development of a Target Statement

A target statement is sometimes called a pro-forma statement, budget or forecast. It is a model (or ideal) of the balance sheet and profit and loss statement. It is ideal because it is one that you wish to achieve. To make a target statement, begin by comparing your balance sheet and profit and loss statement percentages with those of your industry or those you wish to achieve.

Shown on pages 103 and 104 is a sample of a balance sheet and profit and loss statement of the XYZ Hardware and Building Supply Company which includes the percentages of all figures. Also listed is the target statement. In the example shown, the percentages of the industry are marked as industry averages (IA). The balance sheet percentages are percentages of the totals of the asset and liabilities columns respectively, shown as CA & FA (total current assets and fixed assets) and LIAB & NW (total liabilities and net worth). The profit and loss statement shows percentage of net sales. Let's assume that the owner wants to compare his or her averages to those of the industry.

Of course, any target could be used instead of the industry averages. From the example, notice that cash and inventory percentages are way out of line. The owner needs to reduce inventory to gain more cash. Note that the total current asset percentages are very close. The difference is in the mix of current assets.

On the liability side, the owner's bills, shown as accounts payable (ACCTS PAY), is lower than the industry average as shown in the percents between the statement percentages and the industry average percents. This could indicate that the owner is not taking full advantage of payment terms and paying bills too early. This can negatively impact cash.

The profit and loss statement also needs adjustment. The cost of goods sold is below industry average, but the expenses could also use realignment. The expenses could also use realignment. For instance, the advertising expense is very low. If increased, it might help promote greater sales, which in turn would lower the inventory and eventually gain some much needed cash. Also the salary expense is too high for the current circumstances.

Once targets are selected, trying different combinations of sales, expenses, etc. should allow you to see what is required to achieve the financial position that is your goal.

Development of a Target Statement (CONTINUED)

Remember that reality-based experience must be used in making target statements. For instance, you probably won't jump 50% in sales or reduce expenses by half overnight. Don't expect instant results when experience tells you this won't happen. Steady progress toward your goal is the answer. Balance your approach. You can't sacrifice one element very long without causing problems somewhere else.

Develop your own target statement by using your balance sheets and profit and loss statements. Place a column on both reports, one for your averages and another column for your targets. Then compare the two. Determine the figures you need to meet your targets for each line item.

The use of ratios and a cash position chart will help you develop your strategy. Your approach should take into consideration the age of your business, the condition of the economy, your competition, and the nature of your business. Things take time, but if you keep your business finances in balance, you will not only survive, you should prosper.

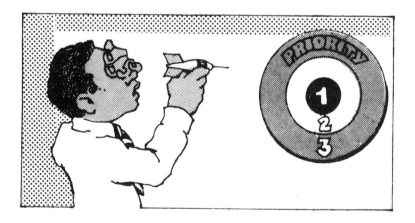

XYZ HARDWARE AND BUILDING SUPPLY BALANCE SHEET YEAR END DATE								
ASSETS		%	IA%*	**LIABILITIES**		%	IA%*
Cash	$ 2,000	.5	7.7	Notes Pay	$18,000	4.3	15.0
Accts Rec	85,00	20.1	33.4	Accts Pay	65,000	15.4	22.5
Inventory	210,000	49.8	33.8	Accruals	95,000	22.5	10.2
Total CA	297,000	70.4	75.9	Total CL	178,000	42.2	47.8
Land/Bldg	50,000			L/T Debt	144,000		
Equipment	50,000			Total LTD	144,000	34.1	21.3
Furn & Fix	25,000			Total Liab	322,000		
Total FA	125,000	29.6	24.1	Net Worth	100,000	23.7	30.9
CA & FA	$422,000	100.0	100.0	Liab & NW	$422,000	100.0	100.0

* IA% = Industry Averages. These percentages are taken from the 1998 Annual Statement Studies, asset size 0-500M, Retailers-Building Material SIC #5211, copyright by Robert Morris Associates, used with permission. Please note the disclaimer and other information in the Appendix.

Explanation of the contents included in the Industry Averages:

Included in Total CA (total current assets) are 1.0% of all other current assets.

Included in Total FA (total fixed assets) are 2.4% intangibles and 4.8% of all other non-current assets.

Included in Total CL (total current liabilities) are current maturing long term debt 7.2%, income tax payables .2%, and all other current liabilities 10.0%.

Included in Liab & NW (liabilities and net worth) are other non-current liabilities 3.9%.

XYZ HARDWARE AND BUILDING SUPPLY
PROFIT AND LOSS STATEMENT
FOR THE YEAR OF (DATE)

		%	IA%*
Net Sales (Less Allow & Discounts)	$700,000	100.0	100.0
Cost of Goods Sold	500,000	71.4	75.2
Gross Profit	200,000	28.6	24.8

EXPENSES		%	IA%*
Salaries	$130,000	18.6	14.7
Freight	7,000	1.0	N/A
Bad Debt	4,000	.6	.3
Utilities	7,000	1.0	.4
Depreciation	4,000	.6	1.0
Insurance	7,000	1.0	.6
Taxes (Local)	8,000	1.1	.2
Advertising	3,000	.4	.7
Interest	10,000	1.4	1.0
Miscellaneous	4,200	.6	4.0**
Total Expenses	**184,200**	**26.3**	**23.0**

		%	IA%*
Operating Income	$15,800	2.3	1.8
Other Income	500	0	.6
Income Before Taxes	$16,300	2.3	2.4

* Expense industry averages are from the 1998 Cost of Doing Business Study, copyright by the National Hardware Association, Indianapolis, IN, used with permission.

** Miscellaneous includes office and shop supplies, building repair and maintenance, rent or ownership in real estate, leasing, legal and accounting, computer services, dues and subscriptions, entertainment, laundry, disposal and other.

Accounts Receivable Aging Schedule

The accounts receivable aging schedule is a control technique that can save you both money and headaches. It is a simple tool. Just keep a record, as shown on page 106, as a reminder of customers who still owe you. A timely follow up, with an appropriate overdue notice to delinquent customers, can head off an account that may be "forgotten" forever.

The table below provides an indication that the longer you wait to collect your accounts receivable, the less likely you are to receive full payment.

This table of collection likelihood for accounts receivable assumes that you have the correct information concerning the address for a customer or the address and a credit check for a business buying finished goods or raw material.

PAST DUE BY:	PROBABILITY OF COLLECTION
30 days	95 percent
60 days	82 percent
120 days	70 percent
6 months	49.5 percent

Reported by John W. Rogers, Professional Credit Manager, Gibson Greeting Cards, Cincinnati, Ohio. Used with permission.

			PAST DUE BY		
CUSTOMER	TOTAL	CURRENT	30-59 DAYS	60-119 DAYS	120-180 DAYS
A	5,000	3,000	2,000		
B	2,000	1,000		1,000	
C	1,000	1,000			
D	4,000	1,000		3,000	
E	3,000	1,000	500	500	1,000
F	12,000	10,000	2,000		
G	3,000	2,000		1,000	
H	5,000	3,000	1,000	1,000	
I	3,000	3,000			
J	2,000	2,000			
K	10,000	10,000			
L	3,000	2,000			1,000
M	7,000	5,000		2,000	
N	2,000	2,000			
O	8,000	7,000	1,000		
P	6,000	3,000	3,000		
Q	6,000		500	4,500	1,000
R	3,000			1,000	2,000
Total	85,000	56,000	10,000	14,000	5,000
Percent	100%	66%	12%	16%	6%

XYZ HARDWARE AND BUILDING SUPPLY
ACCOUNTS RECEIVABLE AGING SCHEDULE

Note: Days refers to calendar not working days.

Summary of Part 6

Check those That You Intend to Use:

❑ A trend analysis is an excellent technique to help me measure the direction my business is going.

❑ A month-by-month and year-by-year comparison will accurately develop the trend my business is taking.

❑ I plan never to run out of cash.

❑ Cash position charting will help me forecast when and how much money I will need to carry out plans.

❑ A target statement is the development of a balance sheet and a profit and loss statement as a "target" which I wish to hit.

❑ The accounts receivable aging schedule is a must if I do credit business.

❑ The accounts receivable aging schedule will help remind me of accounts that are past due and require special attention.

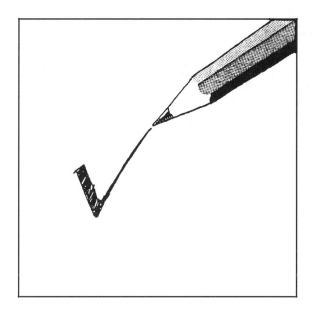

Appendix

Listed below are several sources for locating your industry ratios and expense percentages. This is not an exhaustive list. Your local or university library, trade association, or Chamber of Commerce may be of further assistance.

Dunn and Bradstreet
Information Services
One Diamond Hill Road
Murray Hill, NJ 07974

Includes statistics in over 800 lines of business SIC#0100-8999.

Robert Morris Associates
One Liberty Plaza
Philadelphia, PA 19103

Includes over 500 lines of business.

Almanac of Business and Industrial Financial Ratios
By Leo Troy, PhD
Prentice Hall
Paramus, NJ 07652

Features IRS data on 4.3 million U.S. corporations; provides 50 performance indicators; highlights operating results for 179 industries.

Interpretation of Statement Studies Figures[1]

RMA recommends that Statement Studies data be regarded only as general guidelines and not as absolute industry norms. There are several reasons why the data may not be fully representative of a given industry:

(1) The financial statements used in the Statement Studies are not selected by any random or statistically reliable method. RMA member banks voluntarily submit the raw data they have available each year, with these being the only constraints: (a) The fiscal year-ends of the companies reported may not be from April 1 through June 29, and (b) their total assets must be less than $100 million.

(2) Many companies have varied product lines; however the Statement Studies categorize them by their primary product Standard Industrial Classification (SIC) number only.

(3) Some of our industry samples are rather small in relation to the total number of firms in a given industry. A relatively small sample can increase the chances that some of our composites do not fully represent an industry.

(4) There is the chance that an extreme statement can be present in a sample, causing a disproportionate influence on the industry composite. This is particularly true in a relatively small sample.

(5) Companies within the same industry may differ in their method of operations, which in turn can directly influence their financial statements. Since they are included in our sample, too, these statements can significantly affect our composite calculations.

(6) Other considerations that can result in variations among different companies engaged in the same general line of business are different labor markets; geographical location; different accounting methods; quality of products handled; sources and methods of financing; and terms of sale.

For these reasons, RMA does not recommend the Statement Studies figures be considered as absolute norms for a given industry. Rather the figures should be used only as general guidelines and in addition to the other methods of financial analysis. RMA makes no claim as to the representativeness of the figures printed in this book.

[1]©1998 by Robert Morris Associates

NOTES

Now Available From

CRISP PUBLICATIONS

Books•Videos•CD-ROMs•Computer-Based Training Products

If you enjoyed this book, we have great news for you. There are over 200 books available in the *50-Minute*™ Series. To request a free full-line catalog, contact your local distributor or Crisp Publications, Inc., 1200 Hamilton Court, Menlo Park, CA 94025. Our toll-free number is 800-442-7477. Visit our website at: CrispLearning.com.

Subject Areas Include:

Management

Human Resources

Communication Skills

Personal Development

Marketing/Sales

Organizational Development

Customer Service/Quality

Computer Skills

Small Business and Entrepreneurship

Adult Literacy and Learning

Life Planning and Retirement

CRISP WORLDWIDE DISTRIBUTION

English language books are distributed worldwide. Major international distributors include:

ASIA/PACIFIC

Australia/New Zealand: In Learning, PO Box 1051, Springwood QLD, Brisbane,
Australia 4127   Tel: 61-7-3-841-2286, Facsimile: 61-7-3-841-1580
ATTN: Messrs. Gordon

Philippines: National Book Store Inc., Quad Alpha Centrum Bldg, 125 Pioneer Street,
Mandaluyong, Metro Manila, Philippines   Tel: 632-631-8051, Facsimile: 632-631-5016

Singapore, Malaysia, Brunei, Indonesia: Times Book Shops. Direct sales HQ: STP Distributors, Pasir Panjang Distrientre, Block 1 #03-01A, Pasir Panjang Rd, Singapore
118480   Tel: 65-2767626, Facsimile: 65-2767119

Japan: Phoenix Associates Co., Ltd., Mizuho Bldng, 3-F, 2-12-2, Kami Osaki,
Shinagawa-Ku, Tokyo 141   Tel: 81-33-443-7231, Facsimile: 81-33-443-7640
ATTN: Mr. Peter Owans

CANADA

Reid Publishing, Ltd., 60 Briarwood Avenue, Mississauga, Ontario, Canada L5G 3N6
Tel: (905) 842-4428, Facsimile: (905) 842-9327
ATTN: Mr. Steve Connolly/Mr. Jerry McNabb

Trade Book Stores: Raincoast Books, 8680 Cambie Street, Vancouver, B.C., V6P 6M9
Tel: (604) 323-7100, Facsimile: (604) 323-2600   ATTN: Order Desk

EUROPEAN UNION

England: Flex Training, Ltd., 9-15 Hitchin Street, Baldock, Hertfordshire, SG7 6A,
England Tel: 44-1-46-289-6000, Facsimile: 44-1-46-289-2417
ATTN: Mr. David Willetts

INDIA

Multi-Media HRD, Pvt., Ltd., National House, Tulloch Road, Appolo Bunder, Bombay,
India 400-039   Tel: 91-22-204-2281, Facsimile: 91-22-283-6478
ATTN: Messrs. Aggarwal

SOUTH AMERICA

Mexico: Grupo Editorial Iberoamerica, Nebraska 199, Col. Napoles, 03810 Mexico, D.F.
Tel: 525-523-0994, Facsimile: 525-543-1173   ATTN: Señor Nicholas Grepe

SOUTH AFRICA

Alternative Books, PO Box 1345, Ferndale 2160, South Africa
Tel: 27-11-792-7730, Facsimile: 27-11-792-7787   ATTN: Mr. Vernon de Haas